# *Endorsements*

Fear, Faith, and Freedom. Breaking Through Life's Struggles With God's Help captures the essence of a pilgrimage, but not just any pilgrimage. Like all journeys, it is the movement "from and towards" something, but more accurately, Someone. The cosmic battle between good and evil, sin and salvation, being lost and then found, is played out in a series of real-life experiences. The harsh realities of personal experience are met with the comfort of SCRIPTURAL PROMISE and PERSONAL REFLECTION. In fact, the book opens with a factual reminder of the Plan of God for every human being. The author places herself into the PLAN, and we watch the unfolding of a GOD STORY playing itself out in real time with a real person. I would invite you to enjoy the read, but that would do serious injustice to the intent. I would rather invite you to wrestle with the read in full assurance that God brings victory out of apparent defeat and brings His beauty to our ashes. This is no airbrushed portrait, but rather a raw and blatantly honest account of human vulnerability and weakness being transformed and fashioned by the Hand of God through Love of Christ and the Power of the Holy Spirit.

- Rev. Ian Fitzpatrick
Retired National Director of the Church of the Nazarene

"The scars from our past can colour the choices of today. God can transform these scars for His Kingdom's glory. The choices become redeemed. Jenn has lived this, and now this book is a must-read for others who need past choices redeemed as well."

- Pastor Keith MacAskill
Led Pastor Jenn to Jesus

One is invited into Jenn Dafoe-Turner's life story, a story of fear, faith, and freedom. Jenn has developed a collection of personal stories featuring major struggles, major setbacks, and major discoveries. All of which led her down the road to miraculous triumphs. In her long journey to freedom by way of Christ, she reflects upon her gratefulness for all the many rich treasures she has acquired through prayer, forgiveness, research, and reconciliation.

Her writing style is easy to read and conveys a powerful message. The structured format is interesting and directive. The reader becomes engaged because a series of reflective question following each chapter provides an opportunity to seek reconciliation, to search one's inner self, and a time of confession if so desired.

Jenn's journey to Christ, her exposition of her own failures, her frailties, her own perceived sinfulness, enduring neglect and abuse, and her confessional self-discovery has led her to the Jerusalem she so desires and so deserves.

God's blessings on Jenn and her writings.

- Robert S.A. Fair

Pastor Jenn's Middle School Principal

"Jenn Dafoe-Turner has written a remarkable devotional book and journal titled *Fear, Faith and Freedom Breaking Through Life's Struggles With God's Help.* If you have struggled with addictions or if you're close to someone who does, you'll find biblical truth, encouragement, wisdom, and freedom as you go through this helpful devotional. Jenn's transparency, combined with solid teaching and outstanding application questions, will help you to experience God's love and healing as you embrace your Heavenly Father. Don't miss it!"

- Carol Kent

Founder & Executive Director of Speak Up Ministries

Speaker & Author of *When I Lay My Isaac Down* (NavPress)

Fear, Faith, and Freedom is a tender, truth-filled invitation to bring your most wounded places into the healing presence of Jesus. With profound vulnerability and theological depth, Jenn courageously shares her redemptive journey—from addiction and abuse to abiding love and bold surrender. As a neuropsychologist and woman of faith, I've seen firsthand how emotional wounds can hijack the brain, keep us in cycles of fear, and rob us of peace. Jenn's testimony powerfully illustrates what science confirms: transformation begins when we renew our minds with truth and root our identity in Christ.

Through vivid storytelling, practical reflection, and Spirit-led insight, this book guides readers into emotional, spiritual, and relational freedom. Each chapter holds space for the messy middle of healing while pointing unwaveringly to the hope found in Jesus. If you're desperate to move beyond shame, silence, or striving, *Fear, Faith, and Freedom* will help you trade fear for faith and bondage for the beautiful liberty of life in Christ.

- Dr. Michelle Bengtson

Board-Certified Clinical Neuropsychologist,

Author of *Hope Prevails, Breaking Anxiety's Grip, and Sacred Scars: Resting in God's Promise That Your Past is Not Wasted*

fear,

faith,

freedom

BREAKING THROUGH
LIFE'S CHALLENGES WITH GOD'S HELP

Jenn Dafoe-Turner

Fear, Faith, and Freedom:
Breaking Through Life's Challenges with God's Help
Copyright © 2025 Jenn Dafoe-Turner

Scriptures marked NLT are taken from the HOLY BIBLE, NEW LIVING TRANSLATION, Copyright© 1996, 2004, 2007 by Tyndale House Foundation. Used by permission of Tyndale House Publishers, Inc., Carol Stream, Illinois 60188. All rights reserved. Used by permission.

Scriptures marked ESV are taken from THE HOLY BIBLE, ENGLISH STANDARD VERSION ® Copyright© 2001 by Crossway, a publishing ministry of Good News Publishers. Used by permission.

Scriptures marked NIV are taken from THE HOLY BIBLE, NEW INTERNATIONAL VERSION ®. Copyright© 1973, 1978, 1984, 2011 by Biblica, Inc.™. Used by permission of Zondervan

ISBN: 978-1-963377-55-2

Abundance Books

Kalamazoo, Michigan

www.abundance-books.com

10 9 8 7 6 5 4 3 2

Printed in the United States of America

Cover design by Barefaced Media

This is a memoir. The events are true to the best of the author's memory. Some names and details have been changed or combined for clarity and privacy.

Library of Congress Control Number: 2025947745

Fear, Faith and Freedom: Breaking Through Life's Struggles with God's Help is dedicated to all the people who have helped shape me into the woman I am today.

To my hubby, Ken. You are still the one! I would choose you again and again to go through this crazy life with. You are the calm to my hyper. You are the light to my darkness. You're the one I can't wait to share all my dreams with and then see them come to pass. Thank you for never giving up on us and for always seeing beyond the chaos of addiction and brokenness. Meeting you was beautiful!

To my children and grandchildren, I love you all so much. I'm so thankful I get to be your mom and meemaw. Each of you has such a unique personality, dreams, and ambitions. I pray you reach every one of them. I pray you never stop looking for the good in the world, and when you can't find it, I pray you be it. Keep taking up space and reaching for the stars.

To my mom, thank you for everything you have done for me. I love you with an everlasting love. You are one of the strongest women I know, and because of you, I have learned what it means to rise again and that I am stronger than I think.

To my stepdad, even though you're no longer with us, I am deeply thankful for the impact you had on my life. He once said to me, "Jennifer, you will never get this day again, so live it well." I try every day to remember this and live it out. It was in his final years of life that I would often hear, "Love you, Daughter." I miss him every day.

To Pastor Keith and Heather MacAskill, thank you for introducing me to the man of Jesus Christ and for discipling me in my first few years as a new Christian. I would not be here if that introduction hadn't been made and the discipleship never occurred. The gift you have been given to listen, encourage, and disciple has made such a difference in my life. I am forever grateful.

Foreword

Some books challenge your thinking. Others stir your emotions. But every once in a while, you come across a book that does something far more rare—it awakens your spirit.

That's what happened when I read Fear, Faith, and Freedom.

This is not just another Christian book filled with feel-good theology or sanitized storytelling. This is a raw, redemptive, and radically honest journey through the valleys and mountaintops of one woman's walk with Jesus—a walk that mirrors what so many of us have faced but felt too ashamed to say out loud.

Jenn doesn't shrink back from the hard truths. She invites us into her real-life battles with addiction, abuse, rejection, identity confusion, and spiritual rebellion—not for the sake of drama or shock, but to showcase the power of God's grace. In a world full of curated snapshots and filtered testimonies, Jenn offers something we desperately need: the whole truth. Not just the Sunday-best version of faith, but the Monday-morning kind—the kind forged in the fire of failure and fanned into flame by divine mercy.

What struck me most was how Jenn tells her story not from the mountaintop looking down, but from alongside the reader, still walking out her calling with humility and hope. That's what makes this book so impactful. It's not written from a place of having "arrived," but from a place of abiding. She doesn't pretend the journey is easy. Instead, she shows us that with God, it's possible. And ultimately, it's worth it.

As a fellow first-generation believer, I resonated deeply with her path. When you come to Christ without a faith foundation or spiritual legacy, it can feel like you're fumbling through the dark with nothing but a whisper from heaven. But Jenn reminds us that a whisper is enough when it's from God. She takes the reader by the hand and gently—but boldly—shows that Jesus is a redeemer of all things. Nothing is too broken. No wound is too deep. No detour is too far gone.

Each chapter in this book is anchored in Scripture, soaked in prayer, and seasoned with sanctified imagination. You'll walk through Holy Week like you've never seen it before. You'll see your own story mirrored in the faithfulness of a God who doesn't flinch at our failures but welcomes us back again and again. You'll find devotionals that feel like balm to your soul and challenges that push you out of complacency and into holy obedience.

But more than anything, you'll find hope—not the flimsy kind that fades when life gets hard, but the kind that holds because life is hard.

I believe this book will be a lifeline for women who feel too far gone, too messed up, or too confused to be used by God. It will also challenge those of us who've been walking with Jesus for a while to remember the power of grace and the beauty of surrender. It will call us back to the truth that our freedom was bought at a high price—and now we get to walk in it, every single day.

So if you're ready to lay down shame and pick up purpose…

If you're tired of striving and ready for surrender…

If you're longing for transformation but don't know where to start…

Start here.

Read this book with an open heart. Highlight it. Weep through it. Pray through it. And let the God who met Jenn in her darkest places meet you in yours.

Because He's not finished with your story.

Not by a long shot.

- Robyn Dykstra

Speaker. Author. Fellow Grace Recipient.

Contents

Ultimate Call

If you had the power to revisit a moment in history, what would it be?

Do you have a favorite day? A favorite era? Is there a person you would like to meet? Has a whole list come to mind, or can you narrow it down?

For me, there are many historical moments to witness, like the day I was born—a smart, lovable cutie changing my parents' lives forever. It would have been monumental to see them filled with joy over my arrival.

I'd also like to hear the nails being pounded as Martin Luther hammered the ninety-five theses onto the church doors or see newly liberated Jewish people walk the street with their heads held high after World War II. It would've been delightful to experience the very first snowfall on Earth. Or what about worshiping Jesus on the day he was born in Bethlehem? What about witnessing the day Billy Graham led his first soul into heaven? There are so many days, but none so great as the days of Holy Week.

Holy Week—a brief span of days that altered the world's course, ushering in a new covenant with God through the death and resurrection of his Son, Jesus. Even now, thousands of years later, its impact reverberates across eternity. I know because it changed me, and it's where everything I wish to share begins. This week is the gateway to transformation. Nothing else fills the void in life like Jesus does. He makes me an overcomer, and the ripple effect of my decision to accept his truth set me on a trajectory of change—a change I was desperate for my whole life.

I won't pretend to know where you are on your spiritual journey with Jesus, but because of the type of book this is, I can assume you are looking to overcome an obstacle in your life. Please let me assure you the gospel of Jesus Christ is the best place to start for life transformation.

The Word of God is alive and active, bringing clarity, breaking through our confusion, and directing us on the best pathway for our lives. Scripture always points us to the truth. We are told the Word tastes like honey on our tongues but turns sour in our stomachs. I want to encourage you with a transformational truth: when it comes to understanding the Word of God, if there is a gap between what we believe and what the Word says, it is our thought processes, beliefs, and actions that need to change to align with the Word. This is hard but liberating because nothing will lead us to the changes we desire or fill the emptiness in our lives like applying the gospel's truth.

The gospel story I am about to share with you changed my life many years ago. The unique thing about this story is, it doesn't matter how many times I read it; it continues to change my life, calling me to become. Become what? I don't know because I am still becoming. I have put the truths of the gospel into a seamless narrative, adding depth and creativity to bring Scripture alive on the page. These additions are carefully designed to enhance readability and flow, bringing clarity to the story while respecting the integrity of Scripture. Every creative addition is endnoted to distinguish these insights from the sacred text, guiding readers along a vivid pathway of understanding that highlights the richness of the biblical story.

The Last Supper[1]

"Rabbi, where do you want us to prepare the Passover meal for you?" one of the disciples asked.

Jesus smiled. "Excellent question. When you get into town, a man carrying a pitcher of water will meet you. You must tell him that the teacher has sent us to prepare the Passover meal, that my hour has come. He will take you upstairs to the upper room of his home, set up our meal there."

Jesus wanted his last supper with his close friends to be perfect because this year would be different; this year, Jesus knew he would be the spotless lamb. The sacrifice for the forgiveness of sins. His hour had come to leave this world and return to his Heavenly Father.

———————

Peter and John arrived in the town, and just as Jesus had said, they were met by a man carrying a pitcher of water. He was a quiet man with a gentle spirit; his deep brown eyes were tender, his hair was graying, and his face was worn, but there was something about him that put the two disciples at ease. It was Peter who spoke first, "Excuse me, sir. The teacher has sent us to prepare the Passover meal. His time has come."

The man's eyes lit up, for the men had arrived that he had been waiting for. He locked gazes with Peter and said, "I have been expecting you. Please come in."

Peter[2] and John followed the man into his home. It was nothing special. It didn't boast of wealth, fame, or prestige. It did, however, boast of love and family. His wife was busy at work in the kitchen, making what smelled like lamb. The disciples heard their stomachs growl as they exchanged simple pleasantries with the plumb cheery woman. They continued to follow the man to the back of the house and up the stairs to the much-anticipated room Jesus had spoken of. As they walked up the stairs, they could hear the creak from their weight on them.

At the top of the steps, they were greeted by the room where they would celebrate the Passover meal with their beloved friend. They had spent every day for the last three years learning from him how to become fishers of men and how to love one another.

They quickly set about dusting off the tables and chairs, putting the plates and cups on the table according to their traditions, so the Passover could be celebrated.

Jesus Washes His Disciples' Feet

Before the Passover celebration, Jesus knew that his hour had come to leave this world and return to his Father. He had loved his disciples during his ministry on earth, and now he loved them to the very end. It was time for supper, and the devil had already prompted Judas, son of Simon Iscariot, to betray Jesus. Jesus knew that the Father had given him authority over everything and that he had come from God and would return to God.

The room had grown quiet, save for the soft rustle of fabric and the flicker of lamplight on the walls. The meal was ready, the bread and wine prepared, but before anyone could begin, Jesus stood.

Without a word, he reached for the hem of his outer robe and pulled it over his head, folding it gently and placing it aside. The quiet deepened. The others watched—confused, maybe unsettled—as their teacher wrapped a towel around his waist. It hung low, the ends brushing his knees like a servant's apron.

He poured water into a basin. The sound—gentle, steady— echoed in the room.

Then he knelt.

John, closest to him, startled slightly as Jesus reached for his feet. Dust clung to the skin, collected from streets and long days under the sun. Jesus cupped the heel with tenderness, guiding the foot into the water. His fingers, strong and calloused from carpentry, worked with a gentleness that spoke louder than any sermon.

The water clouded with dirt. With each stroke of the towel, grime vanished into the cloth. Jesus didn't flinch. He washed. He dried. He moved to the next.

No one spoke.

When he reached Peter, the disciple jerked back, his face flushed with alarm. "Lord, are you going to wash my feet?"

Jesus glanced up—eyes calm, steady. "You don't understand now what I am doing, but someday you will."

Peter shook his head, a mix of reverence and resistance flashing in his eyes. "No," he whispered. "You will never wash my feet."

Jesus stayed kneeling, still holding the basin. "Unless I wash you," he said softly, "you won't belong to me."

Silence. Then a breathless reply. "Then—not just my feet, Lord. My hands and my head too."

A smile tugged at Jesus's lips. He shook his head gently. "Those who have bathed need only to wash their feet; their whole body is clean." He paused, pressing the towel to Peter's heel. "But not every one of you."

The towel, now heavy with water and dust, clung to Jesus's waist. As he moved from one disciple to the next, the room remained hushed, reverent.

Each pair of feet held a story—calluses from journeys taken, dirt from paths walked, scars from burdens carried. And still, he knelt before them all. The One who walked on water now knelt on stone.

By the time he rose, his knees were damp, his hands wrinkled, the towel stained with the dust of a dozen roads.

But the feet?

Clean.

And their hearts—though they didn't fully understand yet—had been touched by something deeper than water.

After washing their feet, he put on his robe again and sat down and asked, "Do you understand what I was doing? You call me 'Teacher' and 'Lord,' and you are right, because that's what I am. And since I, your Lord and Teacher, have washed your feet, you ought to wash each other's feet. I have given you an example to follow. Do as I have done to you. I tell you the truth, slaves are not greater than their master. Nor is the messenger more important than the one who sends the message. Now that you know these things, God will bless you for doing them."

Jesus Predicts His Betrayal

Then at the proper time, Jesus sat down with his twelve disciples. He looked at the men sitting with him, eating their supper, and he said, "I tell you the truth, one of you will betray me."

The oxygen was sucked out of the room with each gasp around the table. Peter was the first to speak, "Is it I, Lord?"

James piped in, "Is it me, Lord?"

John, the disciple Jesus loved, choked out, "Lord, please say it isn't me. I just couldn't bear it."

He replied, "One of you who has just eaten from this bowl with me will betray me. For the Son of Man must die, as the Scriptures declared long ago. But how terrible it will be for the one who betrays him. It would be far better for that man if he had never been born!"

Judas, the one who would betray him, also asked, "Rabbi, am I the one?"

And Jesus told him, "You have said it."

As they were eating, Jesus took some bread and blessed it. Then he broke it in pieces and gave it to the disciples, saying, "Take this and eat it, for this is my body, broken for you."

And he took a cup of wine and gave thanks to God for it. He gave it to them and said, "Each of you drink from it, for this is my blood, which confirms the covenant between God and his people. It is poured out as a sacrifice to forgive the sins of many. Mark my words—I will not drink wine again until the day I drink it new with you in my Father's kingdom."

Then they sang a hymn and went out to the Mount of Olives.

Jesus Predicts Peter's Denial

The singing stopped, and the air stilled. Jesus doubled his stride to get a few steps ahead of his friends. He turned and began walking backwards so he could see their faces as he said to them, "Tonight, all of you will desert me. The Scriptures will be fulfilled when it says, 'God will strike the Shepherd, and the sheep of the flock will be scattered.' But after I have been raised from the dead, I will go ahead of you to Galilee and meet you there."

Peter was crushed. How could Jesus say that? Peter declared, "Even if everyone else deserts you, I will never desert you."

Jesus replied, "I tell you the truth, Peter—this very night, before the rooster crows, you will deny three times that you even know me."

"No!" Peter insisted. "Even if I have to die with you, I will never deny you!" And all the other disciples vowed the same.

Jesus Prays in Gethsemane

Then Jesus went with them to the olive grove called Gethsemane, and he said, "Sit here while I go over there to pray." He took Peter and the sons of Zebedee, James and John, and he became anguished and distressed. He told them, "My soul is crushed with grief to the point of death. Stay here and keep watch with me."

He went on a little farther and bowed with his face to the ground, praying, "My Father! If it is possible, let this cup of suffering be taken away from me. Yet I want your will to be done, not mine."

Then he returned to the disciples and found them asleep. He said to Peter, "Couldn't you watch with me for even one hour? Keep watch and pray, so that you will not give in to temptation. For the spirit is willing, but the body is weak!"

Then Jesus left them a second time and prayed, "My Father! If this cup cannot be taken away unless I drink it, your will be done." When he returned to them again, he found them sleeping, for they couldn't keep their eyes open.

So he went to pray a third time, saying the same things again. Then he came to the disciples and said, "Go ahead and sleep. Have your rest. But look—the time has come. The Son of Man is betrayed into the hands of sinners. Up, let's be going. Look, my betrayer is here!"

Jesus loved them deeply, despite knowing this hour would come and that his time with them was short. Every journey, teaching, and act of mercy was intentional, as was every measure of rebuke. He poured himself out like a love offering to them—a gift of deep sacrifice, action, and kindness.

The branches on the olive trees cracked, making way for Judas, flanked by religious leaders and Roman soldiers. Jesus rose, his eyes scanning the scene before finding their mark—Judas's steely gaze.

Judas held Jesus's gaze and stepped forward; his hands trembled as he clutched Jesus's upper arms, leaning in to kiss him, as a friend would do. The warmth of betrayal brushed Jesus's cheek.

"Go ahead, my friend," Jesus whispered. "Do what you came to do."

The Roman guards were quick to move from behind Judas. He sidestepped out of the way, and the guards grabbed Jesus's wrist.

The disciples had been caught off guard and now jumped to action. "Lord, should we fight? We brought the swords!" Wielding his sharp blade, Peter struck at one of the high priest's slaves, whose ear fell to the ground.

"Don't resist anymore," commanded Jesus. "Put your sword away. Those who live by the sword will die by the sword." Jesus shook off the soldier's grip, picked up the ear, reached out his hand, and, with a touch, healed the wounded man.

Jesus turned to the mob—a mix of priests, temple guards, and leaders—his voice calm yet resolute. "Am I a dangerous criminal that you come armed with swords and clubs? Why didn't you arrest me in the temple? I was there every day. But now, this is your hour—when darkness reigns."

"Jesus of Nazareth," the head of the Roman guard said, "you're under arrest."

The guard wrenched Jesus's arms to the front of his body, clapping them together, palm to palm, binding his wrists with a thick rope. He secured the other end to his own belt, dragging Jesus behind him toward the high priest's house. A growing crowd trailed behind.

"Liar."

"Blasphemer."

"Drunkard," they hissed.

Caiaphas

Caiaphas[3] scrutinized the crowd. *Who in this sea of people will be good Jews today and back me up?* Then his eyes fell on Delilah, a close relative of Judas Iscariot. "Of course." He hastened his steps toward her.

"Delilah, how are you?"

"I am well." A smile burst forth. Her eyes grew big, and her voice rose an octave. "And you. How are you, Caiaphas?"

"I am well." His charming smile flashed. "But you know what, Delilah, I could be better, and I think you could help me with my problem."

"Of course, Caiaphas. I'd be honored to help. What do you need?" Delilah had heard her family talking about this man's influence on Judas lately, and she didn't want to miss out on the blessing. If he could help Judas, then he could help anyone. She could trust Caiaphas.

"I want you to tell a story about Jesus to the council. I don't want that blasphemer released. He is causing trouble wherever he goes."

"Bu-bu-but, Caiaphas, that doesn't sound like Jesus." She stumbled over her words. "Are you talking about Jesus of Nazareth?"

"Yes, I'm sure. And remember, the favor is for me." Disgust dripped off his tongue. "Today, someone needs to be released from prison, and it can't be that dog, Jesus."

Delilah heard everything Caiaphas didn't say. The hairs on her arms stood at attention. "I-I-I will say whatever you want."

"No, not what I want but the truth." At that, Caiaphas grasped one of Delilah's hands, did an about-face, and marched off, leading her toward Annas.

"Go on, tell him, Delilah," Caiaphas demanded, raising his voice to be heard over the crowd.

The high priest, who sat dressed in his regalia, frowned. "Tell me what?"

Delilah kept her gaze on the floor. She didn't want to make eye contact with Jesus, who wobbled beside the high priest. "Jesus is a drunkard. He caused a riot at our farm. He spreads lies and tells people he is God."

The crowd erupted. "Crucify him!"

"He's demon possessed," one shouted.

While another yelled, "Crucify him."

The high priest stood, waving his hand.

The crowd silenced.

His gaze was lost in the sea of faces staring back at him. He turned his head to face Jesus. "Well, aren't you going to say anything about these charges?"

Jesus's hands were stretched before him. His legs swayed. He looked straight ahead, his jaw chiseled and shoulders awkwardly squared. He said nothing. Vulnerable to the hour for which he came.

The high priest lunged at him, pointing his finger in his face. "I demand in the name of the Living God that you tell us if you are the Messiah, the Son of God."

Jesus replied, "Yes, it is as you say. And in the future, you will see me, the Son of Man, sitting at God's right hand in the place of power and coming back on the clouds of heaven."

"Blasphemy." The high priest grabbed his robe at the seams of the shoulder and pulled. "Why do you need other witnesses? You have heard it all right here. What is your verdict?"

"Guilty!" the angry mob yelled.

"He must die."

"Crucify him!"

Peter

Peter[4] stood in the courtyard, bitter cold gnawing at his skin. His hands, rough and calloused from years at sea, hovered over the fire, trying to absorb its fleeting warmth. But no heat could thaw the chill that gripped his heart. The flames flickered before him, their dance pulling him into memories—sweet, agonizing memories—of the man he had sworn to follow.

"Come, follow me, and I will make you fishers of men."

The words echoed in Peter's mind, a distant reminder of the moment that had changed everything. Everything. Jesus had invited him out of a simple life, teaching him to embrace his purpose and stand boldly for the kingdom. Now, every breath Peter took felt like a betrayal.

His chest heaved as he sobbed. Hot tears streaked his weathered face, falling unnoticed into the dust. He hunched his shoulders, pulling his cloak tighter around him, trying to disappear into the shadows. If only he could hide from the guilt gnawing at his soul.

A servant girl's voice cut through the night, sharp and accusing. "You were one of those with Jesus, the Galilean."

Her words struck Peter like a blow. His mouth went dry, and for a moment, he couldn't speak. When the words finally came, they were laced with bitterness, the taste of deceit heavy on his tongue. "No…I wasn't with him."

She wasn't convinced. Her eyes narrowed, and she stepped closer. "Yes, you were. I saw you with him."

Peter's heart pounded. Every instinct told him to run, but his legs were rooted to the spot. He shook his head, more forceful this time. "No, you're mistaken. It wasn't me."

The girl's voice grew louder, insistent. "It was you! I saw you!"

Bile rose in Peter's throat, the bitter taste stinging his lips as the words tumbled out. "I swear, it wasn't me!"

And then it came—the sound that shattered him.

Cock-a-doodle-doo. The rooster's cry pierced the cold night air, echoing in Peter's ears like the crack of thunder.

He froze, every muscle in his body locking as Jesus's words rushed back, as clear and sharp as if spoken just moments before. "Before the rooster crows, you will deny me three times."

Pain shot through Peter's chest, radiating outward until it consumed him. His heart pounded wildly, and his legs buckled beneath him. Stumbling back from the fire, he turned and fled, his feet barely keeping pace with the torrent of shame that drove him.

Coward.

The word slithered through his mind, wrapping around him like chains. How could he have fallen so far? How could he have betrayed the one who had invited him to live a new life, who had loved him, trusted him? He ran, the night swallowing his sobs, but no distance could free him from the weight crushing his soul.

Just let me die.

***

Jesus stood before Pilate, his body bruised and broken from the night's violence. His back was hunched, twisted unnaturally from the repeated blows, but still, he stood as tall as his strength would allow. Each breath came slowly, painfully, yet his face remained serene, even in the face of hatred.

The leading priests and religious leaders surged forward. One shouted, "This man has been leading our people to ruin," his eyes gleaming with malice.

"He tells them not to pay taxes to the Roman government and claims he is the Messiah—a king!" The accusation hung in the air, thick with spite. Hatred seeped from every word, relentless and burning.

The crowd shifted uneasily, eyes darting from Jesus to Pilate. They waited—some with curiosity, others with loathing. Pilate stood at a distance, arms folded, his face set in a mask of indifference, but his eyes betrayed a flicker of interest. He turned toward Jesus, sizing him up.

"Are you the King of the Jews?" Pilate demanded, his voice heavy with expectation.

The courtyard seemed to hold its breath as Jesus, battered and silent, finally spoke. His words, though soft, pierced the moment like a blade. "Yes, it is as you say."

Pilate's gaze lingered on him, searching for any sign of rebellion, of guilt. But there was none. This man standing before him, though bruised and bloodied, seemed unshaken, almost regal. Pilate's brow furrowed as he turned to the religious leaders.

"I find nothing wrong with this man!" Pilate's voice cut through the crowd's murmurs.

The council stirred, their desperation growing, fists clenched at their sides. "But he's causing riots everywhere he goes! From Galilee to Jerusalem, he's stirring up trouble!"

Pilate's eyes narrowed at the mention of Galilee. "Oh, is he a Galilean?" The corner of his mouth twitched in slight amusement.

"Yes."

Pilate straightened, a look of relief flashing across his face. "Well then, send him to Herod Antipas. Galilee is his jurisdiction, and Herod happens to be in Jerusalem right now."

Herod was delighted at the opportunity to see Jesus. He had heard about him and hoped to see him perform a miracle.

"Do you know why you're here?" Herod began.

Jesus said nothing. He stood as square as he could, matching Herod's stare.

"Have you heard the accusations?" Herod asked with a little more gumption in his voice.

Jesus didn't move.

"Did you lead a revolt?"

Jesus remained silent.

One of the guards piped up, "Cat got your tongue?"

"Yeah, no wise words today," said another.

One of the guards picked up a royal robe and flung it on Jesus.

A big belly laugh overtook Herod. "Send him back to Pilate. I got nothing on him."

Upon seeing the return of Jesus and hearing Herod's verdict, Pilate gathered the leading priests and other religious leaders, along with the people. "You brought this man to me, accusing him of leading a revolt. I have examined him thoroughly on this point in your presence and find him innocent. Herod came to the same conclusion and sent him back to us. Nothing this man has done calls for the death penalty. So, I will have him flogged, but then I will release him."

In one voice, the crowd roared, "Kill him, and release Barabbas to us!"

Waving his hands to quiet them, Pilate argued, "What has he done?" but his question was silenced with their chants. "Crucify him! Crucify him!"

Pilate raised his hand, silencing them. "Why? What crime has he committed? I have found no reason to sentence him to death. I will, therefore, flog him and let him go."

The angry mob yelled louder and louder. "Crucify him! Crucify him!"

This is going nowhere. If I release Jesus, the crowd will revolt, even though he is innocent. If I don't release him, then I will have an innocent man's blood on my hands. No, I can't have that. I will have to wash my hands of his blood. Perhaps I can settle the crowd if I order him flogged with a lead-tipped whip. In any case, he will die. It is better for him to die like this than by an angry mob.

"Bring me a bowl filled with water," he said. His servants brought him a bowl. He plunged his thick hands into the water and declared before the angry mob, "I am innocent of this man's blood. The responsibility is yours. I order this man be flogged with a lead tip." *If there is a God, maybe he will die before the flogging is finished.*

The Roman guards circled around Jesus, striking him. The blows mercilessly forced his already bruised body to wither. Each hit was more savage than the last. They mocked him with a crown of twisted thorns, pressing it into his scalp. They watched as the blood flowed down his face. Despite the unbearable pain and the weight of their scorn, Jesus remained silent, his eyes full of compassion and strength. The guards, driven by hatred and power, continued their assault, unaware they were striking the very Son of God, who bore their violence without retaliation, embodying the ultimate sacrifice for mankind.

The guards put a reed stick in Jesus's hand like it was a gold scepter and kneeled before him. "Hail the King of the Jews." Their spit slid down his torn flesh as they grabbed the stick out of his hand. They beat him on the head and laughed as the blood ran down his body.

You could hear the wind with each crack of the whip as his flesh tore open and the blood poured out. *Crack! Crack! Crack!*

"Thirty-nine and forty," the guard counted. "Halt. No more."

The guard grasped a piece of Jesus's robe and ripped it away from Jesus's torn flesh. Pieces of the robe flew with chunks of flesh, leaving Jesus naked and vulnerable. "Get up, Nazareth, or should I say, 'King of the Jews.'"

***

Pilate emerged once more. His face was pale, his eyes shadowed, his jaw tight with frustration. In the stillness, his voice rang out, sharp and deliberate. "I am bringing him out to you," he declared, motioning toward the entry. "But know this, I find him not guilty."

The soldiers led Jesus forward.

A hush fell over the crowd as they beheld Him. The crown of thorns pressed into his brow sent rivulets of blood down his face. The purple robe, draped mockingly over his torn back, clung to his wounds. His hands trembled slightly, yet his gaze was steady. Unshaken.

Pilate gestured to the broken man beside him. "Behold the man!"

For a heartbeat, no one moved.

Then.

Chaos erupted.

"Crucify him!" shrieked a voice from the priests' circle.

"Crucify him!" others echoed, fists raised, mouths curled in hatred.

Pilate flinched, stepping back as if the venom in their words had struck him. He looked to the robed leaders, disbelief flashing in his eyes. "Take him yourselves and crucify him," he snapped, the sarcasm not fully masking the dread in his tone. "I find no guilt in him."

The priests surged forward, their voices hardening. "By our law, he must die," one barked, "because he claimed to be the Son of God."

At those words, something shifted in Pilate's face—his defiance cracked into fear. His throat bobbed. Without a word, he turned on his heel and disappeared, dragging Jesus behind him.

Inside, the torchlight flickered against stone walls, casting long shadows. Pilate spun to face Jesus, his voice lower now, edged with urgency.

"Where are you from?" he demanded.

Jesus stood silent, gaze calm, lips closed.

Pilate's voice rose. "Will you not speak to me?" He stepped closer, gesturing wildly. "Don't you realize I have the authority to release you—or crucify you?"

Jesus finally spoke, voice steady and sorrowful. "You would have no authority over me at all unless it had been given to you from above. Therefore, the one who handed me over to you has the greater sin."

Pilate stepped back, shaken. His shoulders tightened as if bearing an invisible weight. He moved toward the door—but the roar outside grew louder.

"If you release this man," a voice thundered from the crowd, "you are no friend of Caesar!"

"He claims to be a king!" another added. "Any man who claims to be king is no friend to Rome!"

Pilate halted in the doorway, jaw clenched. His eyes darted toward the soldiers—then to Jesus—and finally to the mob outside. Their fury was unrelenting, rising like a wave determined to drown reason.

Moments later, he climbed the stone steps of the judgment platform, Gabbatha, and sat on the seat of decision. He stared into the mass of shouting faces, raising one hand to call for silence.

"Behold—your King!" he announced, voice strained.

"Away with him!" the people screamed.

"Crucify him!"

Pilate leaned forward. "Shall I crucify your King?"

The priests stepped out of the crowd, their eyes like flint. "We have no king but Caesar!"

Silence fell again heavy and grim.

Pilate's shoulders slumped, and he nodded to the guards.

Without another word, he handed Jesus over to be crucified.

One guard yelled at Jesus, "It's time to take your final walk, Messiah."

The Roman guards made Jesus carry his cross with blood pouring down his body, barely able to walk, to Golgotha.

The wooden cross landed with a thud, causing the dust to fly. The guard pushed Jesus down beside it. The guard's eyes were cold. No emotion whatsoever. "Get on that cross, you dirty dog."

Jesus managed to shimmy his broken, torn-open body a smidge.

"You getting lazy, are ya?" The guard picked up his battered body and threw it on the hard, wooden beam.

Jesus's eyes squeezed open, and he gasped for breath. The wood splinters dug into his flesh. Blood oozed.

The guards wrenched one of his arms out to the side and drove the first nail in. His cry could be heard over the crowd, causing a silence to fall as they anticipated the second nail and then, the third. Each scream was more shrill than the last.

"Men, where is the sign Pilate wants to be put over his head?"

Another guard brought it over. "I got it." He hammered it above Jesus's head.

It read, "The King of the Jews."

"Grab your post, boys. We're going to lift it into place."

The soldiers secured their spots. They grabbed hold of the rope and walked forward, erecting Jesus to be displayed as a common criminal for all to see.

As Jesus hung there, sweat and drops of blood fell from his body. The foul stench rose.

The soldiers gave him wine mixed with bitter gall, but Jesus refused to drink it.

Two others, both criminals, were led out to be executed with him—one on his right and one on his left.

Jesus said, "Father, forgive them, for they don't know what they are doing." And the soldiers gambled for his clothes by throwing dice.

The crowd watched, and the leaders scoffed. "He saved others," they said, "let him save himself if he is really God's Messiah, the Chosen One."

The soldiers mocked him too. They bellowed, "If you are the King of the Jews, save yourself!"

One of the criminals hanging beside him scoffed. "So you're the Messiah, are you? Prove it by saving yourself—and us, too, while you're at it!"

But the other criminal protested. "Don't you fear God even when you have been sentenced to die? We deserve to die for our crimes, but this man hasn't done anything wrong." Then he said, "Jesus, remember me when you come into your kingdom."

"I assure you, today you will be with me in paradise."

At noontime, the sky went dark.

The chatter faded into the distance, the people drifted out of sight, and his world went black. Around 3:00 p.m., Jesus yelled, "My God, my God, why have you forsaken me?" Then he yelled out again and gave up his spirit.

The earth shook, rocks split apart, and tombs opened. A violent earthquake followed. Cracks spread like spiderwebs across the ground, and buildings trembled as if shivering in the cold. In the temple, the sacred curtain, a rich fabric that separated the Holy of Holies from the rest of the sanctuary, ripped apart from top to bottom. It was as if an invisible hand had torn it, symbolizing that the barrier between God and man had broken.

As Jesus's last cry echoed through the darkened land, the spectators stood paralyzed, their faces pale against the sudden nightfall. The once-raucous crowd fell into stunned silence, their scornful laughter replaced with gasps of disbelief and whispers of fear. Even the soldiers, hardened by countless battles, looked at each other with wide-eyed alarm, their mocking smirks wiped clean.

The earth held its breath as if in mourning...

Nicodemus came and took his lifeless body off those shameful pieces of wood to put him in the tomb. Mary watched them seal the tomb. It was over. Her Lord was gone, and it was all she could do to pull herself away from the tomb to go home.

Silent Saturday

The next day was a fog. Nobody really talked. It was Passover, a time to celebrate God's salvation of his children from the hand of Pharaoh. But today, there was no celebration, only numbness and sadness. A day filled with going through the motions because Mary of Bethany couldn't get the images of what she had seen the day before out of her mind.

Mary could hardly believe the events she had witnessed over the last few days. All her hope had been drained. Jesus, her Lord, her friend, had been brutally beaten beyond recognition.

She tried to think back to good memories. She forced her mind to remember the times he had come for dinner. She loved sitting at his feet, listening and learning. "Tell me more, rabboni," she would say.

Only recently, Jesus had been at their home, and Mary had anointed his feet with nard. She let out a little giggle when she thought about the uproar she caused among the men who were there, but Jesus had told them that what she had done would be remembered "wherever the gospel is preached." She had felt so honored because Jesus accepted her gift to him, but now realized she had received the greater gift, preparing his body for burial. *Oh, Jesus, my Lord. Why? I love you. I miss you.*

With tears pooling in the corners of her eyes, the memories kept coming. She wanted this pain to end, but she knew it would only end when she could see her Lord alive and well.

What was she going to do?

The image of his lifeless body overwhelmed her with the soberness of knowing he would never again smile or say her name or wrap his arms around her.

———

Sunday morning was the third day.

Did that really happen? Mary Magdalene's last thought before bed was her first thought this morning. *No. God, why?* Putting one foot in front of the other, Mary willed herself to get ready. She would do the only thing she could think of to feel better—go to the tomb.

When she got there, Mary gasped. The stone that had sealed the tomb only two days before was rolled away.

Mary ran back to town to the disciples, screeching till she reached them.

"Simon Peter. He is not there."

"John, he is gone."

"Matthew, did you take him?"

Simon Peter took off running, yelling over his shoulder, "I have to see this for myself. Could it be?"

Mary made her way back to the tomb with others. There was chatter all the way. What could this mean? How could it be? Who took him? Where did they take him? Why would they take him? Questions and more questions were all they had.

Mary's grief continued in waves. Hot tears made their way down sunken trails on her face. Her Lord was gone. The tomb was empty. As she stooped over to look for Jesus, through her tear-blurred vision, she caught the sight of a glittering. The most spectacular angels robed in dazzling white sat inside the tomb, one where her Lord's head should have been and one where his feet should have been; the brilliance of their robes glistened through the flood of tears.

"Why are you crying?" they asked with tenderness in their voices, offering Mary no comfort.

Through gut-wrenching sobs, she said, "They have taken my Lord, and I don't know where they have put him."

Her pain was overwhelming, and she couldn't stand to look at the grave that had once held her Lord any longer; she turned her head. Through her muddled vision, she saw someone approach. The man could see her agony, and he looked upon her with tenderness. "Why are you crying? Whom are you looking for?"

Mary, unsure of the man's identity, perhaps a gardener, had a glimmer of hope. Maybe, just maybe, he knew where her Lord was. He might have even taken him. "Sir, if you have taken him away, tell me where you have put him, and I will go and get him."

"Mary," the man said.

That was all it took; she knew as soon as he spoke her name that it was her Lord, Jesus. She squealed with delight. "Teacher." She ran to him and wrapped her arms around him.

His eyes filled with an unutterable love. His wounds were gone, replaced with scars that had a heavenly glow, as if they emanated from within him. His resurrection was not simply a return to earthly life, but a victory over death itself, a testament to his divine nature.

In the days that followed, Jesus appeared to his disciples, sharing meals, teaching, filling their hearts with joy and their minds with understanding. They touched his hands and his side, their doubts melting away in the face of the living proof of his resurrection. Jesus, their Lord and friend, was alive. He conquered death, just as he had promised. The crucifixion was not the end of the story but the beginning of a new covenant, a testament to God's undying love for humanity.

The gospel of Jesus is what each choice in the following chapters is about. Without the gospel, we would be eternally lost, but with this foundation firmly in place, we can rise above. Each day, we are asked to die to ourselves and live for Christ. This can only be accomplished when we stand firmly on the truth found in his Word.

Gentle Challenge

Reflect on this profound moment in history and ask yourself: Have I truly grasped the significance of Jesus's resurrection, his victory over death? Am I living in the light of his love, sacrifice, and triumph? Take a moment to examine your own heart. Are you living out the teachings that Jesus imparted to his disciples—the message of love, forgiveness, and salvation that he embodied? It's a challenge to live a life worthy of his sacrifice. This is not a call for perfection, but a gentle prompting toward a path filled with love, forgiveness, and understanding. You will stumble and fall, but let every fall be a reminder, not of your weakness, but of his strength and his promise of redemption. It's a gentle challenge, but its rewards are eternal.

Reflection Questions

1. How does the story of Jesus's resurrection impact your perspective on life and death?

2. In what ways can we embody Jesus's teachings in our daily interactions and relationships?

3. How can we turn our stumbling blocks into stepping stones, using our falls as reminders of his strength and redemption?

Fear, Faith, and Freedom

Journal Your Thoughts Here

Pray with Me:

Dear heavenly Father,

We come before you today with hearts filled with gratitude for the sacrifice of your Son, Jesus Christ. We are humbled by the immense love demonstrated through his crucifixion and resurrection, forever reminding us of the victory over death and the promise of eternal life. Lord, help us to internalize the significance of these events and to live our lives as a reflection of the love, forgiveness, and salvation Jesus embodies. Guide us to be more like him in our daily interactions and relationships, to turn stumbling blocks into stepping stones, and to find strength in his redemption. We pray our lives honor his sacrifice, and we continually strive to walk in his path of love and understanding.

In Jesus's name, we pray.

Amen.

Scripture Memory Verse

The reward for trusting him will be the salvation of your souls.

1 Peter 1:9 NLT

Chapter One

The Walk to a Better Life

"The sign of Jonah. What the heck was the sign of Jonah?" This question burned in my mind as I woke up from a night of interrupted sleep. I hurried to get out of bed. I needed a cigarette, coffee, and my Bible before the kids got up to greet the day with all their energy.

I made my way to the kitchen. Sleeping on a pullout couch in the living room had its advantages. I could sneak into the kitchen without waking the kids, giving me time to sit at the table and read. I clicked the button on the kettle, put the coffee crystals in the cup, and inhaled the rich, heavenly aroma. *If God has a smell, I'm sure it's this.*

With my heavenly brew secured, sitting at the table, I opened my old Bible I had from years before to the Gospel of Matthew, to chapter twelve, which is about the sign of Jonah. I read with fresh eyes, hoping to understand better. However, I remained mystified and stumped. *Thank God it's Sunday. I can ask the pastor when we get to church.*

Life was so hectic with our four little ones running about that I loved to put the kids in the buggy and walk to Sunday services. With the morning rush over, we stepped outside. The morning sun invited us to play along the path to the church.

Over the previous few months, I had grown to like this little church and its people. From the time we had our new daughter dedicated, warmth greeted me each time I opened the door, even when no one was there. The piano player made the keys sing a love song directly toward the throne of Jesus. It was heaven on earth.

Walking through the double glass doors to the foyer of the little building, I was eager to have a conversation with my pastor. I wanted to know about Jonah's sign. For as long as I had been attending, I read my Bible, trying to make sense of the words because I knew they had meaning and life. These words had the power to bring comfort. I knew because I had felt their influence and security.

I got myself and my baby boy comfy in what was soon becoming my spot in the back corner of the sanctuary. Bo loved looking at the Christmas decorations adorning the small sanctuary. The green wreaths were tied with his favorite color ribbon, Christmas red. They hung uniformly on each window. The stained glass glistened behind the wreaths, causing the sun to dance differently on the walls.

I was delighted watching his eyes grow with amusement, watching the color bounce around while I secretly wished for the day I would be ready to follow Christ. I was still a big old sinner, and I knew it. I just had a few things I needed to clean up first. I needed to stop swearing, smoking, and drinking. I needed to be a better mom. I needed to get rid of my anger. I knew I was messed up from years of abuse, but if I could clean myself up, then I could present myself to Jesus all shiny and new.

Satan had me right where he wanted me, believing I had to do all this work on my own. This is one of the biggest lies of the enemy, and I fell for it. Hook, line, and sinker. He didn't want me to go to Jesus. He wanted me to stay trapped in denial, disobedience, and destruction. He comes to kill, steal, and destroy. He offers death, but it comes disguised as a relief.

Christ came to give life abundantly. To access this life, I first had to commit my life to him. I was adopted into the family of God by confessing with my mouth that Jesus is Lord and by believing he is the Christ. The one who came to take away the world's sins. This belief is the foundation for overcoming everything. I believe there is a level of healing we can only attain with Jesus. We can find some relief and coping mechanisms, but the depth of healing Jesus wanted in my life could only be done with him.

Before the service started, the pastor came and sat on the edge of the pew in front of my friend and me and turned toward us. "Good morning, ladies."

I politely let my friend say good morning, but she knew I was anxious to talk to him. As I bounced Bo on my lap, I said, "I know you only have a few minutes, but I was reading last night, and I couldn't figure out what the sign of Jonah is. Who is Jonah? What do I need to know about him?"

My pastor's eyes lit up. "What great questions. I wish you hadn't asked me five minutes before the service starts, but quickly, the sign of Jonah is like Jesus being in the tomb for three days because Jonah was in the belly of the whale for three days. Jonah was a prophet, and you should probably learn about him. Do you want to talk next week?"

"Yes. If you don't mind."

"Not at all. I will call you." With that he stood up to make his way to the platform to begin the service.

In a few moments, the church came alive with worship. "Joy to the World" vibrated in my chest as I joined my voice to the mighty chorus. I was hungry for Jesus and, sitting in the most unholy spot, I was painfully aware of how hungry I was. I longed to be good enough. I called it the most unholy spot for this reason: It was the quick getaway spot, closest to the exit door. I didn't have to engage in conversation. I didn't have to speak to anybody if I didn't want to. I knew I was sinful, and my life didn't measure up to the words of Scripture.

On that morning, however, the words of the message cut right to the core of my heart. The words, "If you feel unworthy, if you feel unwanted, and like you will never measure up," hit me in all the right ways. It was like the pastor had a scope and could see into my thoughts.

"If you want a new life, today is the day of salvation, and you can have it."

Boy. You have no idea how much I want that life, but I am not ready. I bounced Bo on my knee, distracting myself from the soon-overwhelming guilt that would creep in to affirm I wasn't good enough. At the end of the service, the pastor gave an altar call, offering a new life in Christ. A fresh start. A do-over, and I wanted it but knew I wasn't there yet.

"It's time, Jennifer." I looked behind me to see who was talking, but no one was there. I looked in the other direction, but no one was there either. Then, I knew it was the voice of the Lord. I was overwhelmed with emotion. I had heard this voice my whole life and thought I was crazy. In my family, I was told it's okay to talk to yourself, but if you answer yourself, it means you're crazy. But it was the voice of the Lord guiding me, reassuring me, and encouraging me on some of the hardest days I ever experienced.

The pastor's words made sense to me in an instant. It wasn't about me. It wasn't about what I could or couldn't do. This grace was a gift, and I only had to receive it.

I passed my sweet boy to my friend and stepped out of the pew. I feared what people would say. *Oh no, people are going to know I'm a sinner,* I thought with each wobbly step I took forward. It seems silly now, but the panic was real at that moment. The exposure of stepping out of the pew to descend the aisle was humbling. I walked the same aisle the day I married my husband, but this day the passageway seemed so long. It was a journey of vulnerability and surrender.

I reached the front of the church and knelt at the altar, as I had seen others do. The pastor knelt next to me and led me in the sinner's prayer as I surrendered my life to Christ.

"Dear God, please forgive me for the sins in my life. I believe you are the ultimate sacrifice. The perfect Lamb of God, you went to the cross where you died a sinner's death in my place. You rose to life three days later, and forty days later, you returned to heaven, preparing a home for us. I believe you are coming back to get us. In Jesus's name, amen."

My body shook from being overcome by the Holy Spirit. The power of the Lord came upon me with such intensity that it was as if I had been plugged into an electrical outlet, and the current was running through my body. This was a life-altering moment, and I was a new person in Christ from this day forward.

I wanted the peace of Christ, but to receive it, I first had to do something with my fear of the ultimate rejection. The sin in my life had created so much fear that it controlled me for quite some time. Scientists[5] say fear is universal to all people. Each person is born into this world with two universal fears: falling and loud noises. As people grow, they develop unique worries based on such factors as their environment, family, and DNA. We all have things we fear.

I feared I would never be loved and never find my spot in life. I feared I would fail as a parent and friend, never measuring up to those around me.

I constantly compared myself to others, and I always came up short. I was afraid to look within because I knew my heart held years of abuse and neglect. My insecurities were high, and my peace was low. Surrendering my life to Christ was like finding water in the desert.

It's safe to say I had deep, debilitating fears that gripped my heart and created ongoing anxiety. Nobody else knew about them, but they were the entrenched phobias I harbored.

The Christmas story can be understood in the context of fear. Christ came in the middle of fear. Zechariah in the temple was gripped with fear at Gabriel's appearance. This same angel appeared to Mary sometime after and frightened her. The angel had to calm her by assuring her there was nothing to be afraid of. The shepherds were out in the field tending their flocks when, suddenly, the sky lit up, and an angel appeared. The glory of the Lord shone around them, and they were terrified.

Is it possible there is a connection between God's glory and people's fear? Romans 3:23 (ESV) says, "For all have sinned and fall short of the glory of God[.]" This verse tells me God's original design for us is to reflect or manifest his glory. When he created Adam and Eve in the Garden of Eden, he made them as human beings to reflect, reveal, and manifest his glory. God designed the world, and he designed people to reflect his image. So, with these thoughts in mind, my reflection should be the glory of God.

But then something happened. Sin entered the world and people's hearts through Adam and Eve in the Garden of Eden. The glory and perfection of God was tarnished, so neither human beings nor the creation in which we live fully reflect God's glory. Sin created distance between the glory of God and the sinfulness of our human existence, and it is this gap—the gap between who we are designed to be and who we know ourselves to be—that creates fear in life.

In Genesis, immediately after Adam and Eve sinned by eating the fruit of the Tree of Knowledge of Good and Evil, they realized they fell short of God's perfect design for them, and they hid in fear. Fear entered the picture with the distance between what God had intended and who Adam and Eve had come to be.

The fear I experience daily results from being aware of this gap—this distance between who I was designed to be and who I am in this fallen world. Before that Sunday morning, I lived in this gap, filled with fear. I believed the lies of the voice of opposition my whole life: I wasn't good enough. I was too sinful ever to be accepted by God. I had too much garbage to clean up. But on that Sunday morning, the Lord broke down the lies spoken over me, which I had always accepted as truth. The "lying truth" is the phrase I use to describe lies spoken over me so much that they become my truth.

After the service, I was hugged by so many people to the point of overwhelm. I stepped out the double glass doors into the early afternoon sun, in all its brilliance, to be greeted by the earthy smell of autumn. My body was still vibrating from meeting Jesus at the altar. I knew something had happened within me. I didn't realize God was preparing my heart to be open to the idea that I was designed for security, productivity, justice, and purpose, and that I had meaning in life.

All I had ever known was a sinful world—a world of injustice, unfairness, loss, failure, and some of that sin and failure was in me. The gap between who God originally designed for me to be and what I experienced as reality created my fear.

This gap created havoc in my relationships. When fear was in control, it created such anxiety about reconciling with someone—about talking to someone and saying, "Hey, listen, I was a little offended by what you did, but let's work this out," or "I apologize for hurting your feelings this way. Would you forgive me?" These interpersonal moments created fear because I, along with the rest of humanity, have been hardwired to understand the standard, the perfect design of God.

God's incredible design is for perfect community, connection, intimacy, and relationship. It's part of who he is. We live in a world impacted by sin, and the reality here includes rejection, gossip, criticism, and anger. I experience these things in relationships with others plagued by this same human condition: sin.

If it were not for sin, I wouldn't have to worry about sickness, pain, failure, injustice, or being taken advantage of. As it is, sin has entered the world and created a gap, filling people with fear.

Fortunately, for this reason, Christ came to overcome sin and its ramifications. He came to conquer our fears. The shepherds learned this as they stood there shaking. The glory of the Lord shone around them. They were in the presence of God's great glory and realized how small they were in comparison. The angel said to them, "Do not be afraid; for behold, I bring you good news of great joy which will be for all the people; for today in the city of David there has been born to you a Savior, who is Christ the Lord" (Luke 2:10–11 NASB). Heaven exploded as soon as the angel announced Christ, a Savior—a solution—had been born. There was an even greater flash of light. An entire multitude of angels appeared, and they began to sing a Christmas carol. The song is short, but it's profound. They sang, "Glory to God in the highest, and on earth peace to men on whom His favor rests" (Luke 2:14 BSB).

This little song holds the solution to our fears. When Christ came into the world, he brought two things. First, he brought glory to God in his coming. God designed the world to reflect his glory and desires the world to reflect the greatness of who he is. Sin entered the picture, tarnishing the world, but God did not abandon his glory. He didn't say, "Well, that plan didn't work out. I'm going to have to choose something else now." No, instead, God chose to restore and redeem his glory in the world, and he did that by sending his Son. The coming of Christ into the world was, first and foremost, to reveal the glory of God.

The blessing of peace is the second gift Christ brought. Christ came to bring glory to his Father and peace to all people. He was not only born to humanity but died for it, and in the life, death, and resurrection, the gap between God and creation was closed. Christ came to change hearts and create a new heart within us. Christ was the plan to restore us to God's original design, and when we live accordingly, we live in peace. A life of peace is only found in a relationship with Jesus Christ, who changes us from the inside out.

My new faith raised this question: If Christ came to restore the glory of God in me so I could live as God intended, what would I do with my fears? I began to think of what I was most afraid of, and if it were removed or changed in my life, then what kind of life could I live? My greatest fear is to be rejected, and my greatest desire is to be accepted.

In surrendering my life to Christ, I began to understand that if I wanted to overcome my fears, I had to let them drive me to Christ because, for years, I let them drive me out of my mind. I would lay awake at night with my thoughts on the spin cycle, wringing my hands. My anxieties would overwhelm me and put my worries on overdrive.

Saul, in the Old Testament, was raised as the first king of Israel, but when he was too afraid to fight Goliath, God used a teenage boy named David instead. Suddenly, the hearts of the people turned to David. They applauded more loudly for him than they did for Saul. Saul began to fear for his position. He was afraid David would overthrow the throne, which was not David's intention. Saul started to do the most irrational things. He chased and attacked David. He criticized and humiliated him. Saul was a man driven by his fears, and he became a maniac.

I did the same thing. I was just like Saul. Overwhelmed by my fears, I become a loose cannon. For years, my fears drove me to do crazy things until I learned to take them to Christ because he was the answer to every fear.

When Jesus died, the disciples were scared to death. And they were equally frightened when he rose from the dead. His first words to his disciples were, "Peace be with you!" (John 20:19 NIV). Christ came to dispel fears and bring peace to life by bridging the gap between the Creator and the created caused by sin.

I have had to think and pray through fears. The fear of inadequacy, of not having what it takes for life. Jesus said to me, "For my divine power has given you everything for life and godliness according to the true knowledge of me who called you by my own purpose and glory. I've given you everything" (2 Peter 1:3 my paraphrase).

He took my fear that my past failures and mistakes make me no longer valuable to God. Jesus said to me, "If you confess your sins, I'm faithful and just to forgive you of your sins and to cleanse you from all unrighteousness" (1 John 1:9 my paraphrase).

When I feared not having a sense of identity, and I wasn't sure who I was or if I was really changed by Jesus, he said to me, "If any person is in Christ, you are a new creation. The old has gone, and the new has come" (2 Corinthians 5:17 my paraphrase).

For many years, I feared I was insignificant—could I ever really be loved and cared for? I had an incredible sense of loneliness in my life. And in his loving-kindness, Jesus said, "Come to me all you who are weary and heavy burdened, and I will give you rest. Come, come, come. Take my yoke upon you because my burden is easy, my yoke is light. Come over here, come into relationship with me and I'll ease that" (Matthew 11:28–30 my paraphrase).

When I was learning to face my fear, I would lay awake at night trying to figure out how to make it all work until one night, the Holy Spirit challenged me with this question: "If you are in me and you trust me like you say you do, in what way does your relationship with me help you to overcome this fear?" I needed to stop my mind from jumping on the hamster wheel and find my answers in the Bible. Christ makes all the difference in the world. I needed to learn to stop letting my fears drive me to this type of irrational behavior, let them move me to Christ, and let him guide me through my fear.

When I surrendered my life to Christ, my fears didn't automatically disappear. I had to learn how to handle those remaining fears through a framework of grace and mercy. I let them drive me to Christ and allow faith to move me forward. As I trust him, he answers my prayers, whether with yes, no, or not right now. God is faithful and is continually transforming my faith in his faithfulness.

I was full of fear because sin in my life created a distance between the glory of God and the frail humanity in me. But Christ bridged the gap, and all my fears are answered in him. He is the one who knows what I'm going through right now and is aware of all my anxieties and has brought me overwhelming peace.

Gentle Challenge

Spend time with the Lord and ask him to search you to reveal anything that needs to be confessed.

Reflection Questions

1. What is an area of fear you currently struggle with?

2. According to Scripture, how will Jesus meet you in this fear?

3. What underlying emotion is tied to this fear?

Journal Your Thoughts Here

Pray with Me:

Dear heavenly Father,

Thank you for your loving-kindness in sending your son Jesus to the cross. He went in our place to overcome sin, death, and the grave. Continue to search me and reveal areas of my life I need to surrender, so I may live in this world free from fear in your overcoming power.

In Jesus's name, we pray.

Amen.

Scripture Memory Verse

If we confess our sins, he is faithful and just to forgive us our sins and to cleanse us from all unrighteousness.

1 John 1:9 ESV

Chapter Two

A New Best Friend

"Oh God, why can't I stop? Why aren't you taking this addiction from me?" I hurled my words upward, my eyes fixed on the dingy yellow ceiling. For the life of me, I couldn't figure out why God wasn't removing my addiction as he had for other people.

Since I became a Christian, I have heard countless accounts of God intervening to say, "You are healed." People have been saved and freed from their addictions.

I longed for this story, but it wasn't mine. No, I struggled daily with smoking. I wanted to quit but felt weak and powerless to overcome the power of the cigarette's seduction. Some days I was more determined than others. I would take a stand. I would cut them up and throw them out, only to have sheer panic wash over me a couple of hours later. *Oh no, what have I done?* Then I would rush to the store to buy them again. At times, I was so desperate for a cigarette that if I didn't have my own, I would smoke cigarette butts.

But one morning, sitting in that stale stench of cigarette smoke, the Lord spoke to my spirit. "How much value does a cigarette hold for you?"

The question made me stop and think. I had never determined before what a cigarette meant to me. I just knew it was always there. I couldn't remember a time when I didn't smoke. With the trail of memories painting their picture in my mind, I recalled my first time getting caught smoking. I was a young girl in grade three.

That day the blue sky held the sun high overhead as I squatted by the church, leaning against the brownstone. I felt safe and secure while nestled behind the evergreen bushes in front of the building. Nobody could see me from the road or walking by. I put my knapsack underneath my bottom so I wouldn't get dirty, and it offered a bit of support.

I reached into my pocket to pull out a new package of cigarettes. The plastic wrap crinkled in my fingers as I took the plastic off. There was nothing like opening a new pack of smokes, freshly stolen from the corner store. The aroma of unburnt tobacco was my favorite smell. It was the precursor to comfort. My little fingers couldn't open the package fast enough to get the cigarette out.

All I could think about since I had opened my eyes that morning was this moment. I fumbled with the matches, taking extra caution not to burn myself again. As I took the first drag, my lungs filled with heavy smoke, and my body instantly calmed. The inhale of the thick smoke brought in peace, and the exhale released all the tension of holding shame from carrying all my secrets.

I felt ready to face the day after having a cigarette. It empowered me. It also helped to know I had more for after school. It made me feel like I was in control and would be okay.

Ring. Ring. Ring. The sound of the school bell let me know it was time to get to school. I stepped out from behind the bush. I didn't want to be late. I could hear the kids playing in the schoolyard, directly behind the church on the other side of the building. I knew when the first bell rang, I had enough time to get to school and get in line from my hiding spot behind the bushes.

As I walked up the street, my third-grade teacher greeted me. "Good morning, Jennifer." She smiled at me. My eyes went big like saucers. I was like a deer caught in the headlights.

My voice cracked. "Good morning." A sense of instant dread washed over me. Whatever peace I had just experienced from a fresh breath of smoke was gone instantly. I had been caught.

At nine years old, in third grade, I was completely addicted to cigarettes. The realization of this truth startled me as my oldest son's cute little face popped into my mind. He was so little and was also going into third grade. I could see the comparison between his childhood and my own. They were very different. He was filled with love and goodness and parents who were bound and determined to make sure he knew he was loved and wanted.

After a few moments of sitting with this memory, the light came on; a cigarette was my best friend. A cigarette never hit me, never called me a name, never abused me, and never condemned me. A cigarette was a constant in my life. It never let me down. It was always there. A cigarette could bring me comfort. If I were angry, a cigarette would calm me down. I was in a committed relationship with a cigarette, and then the Father showed me the most profound thing: even though smoking had never hurt me, it was slowly killing me. This is Satan's deception; he promises one thing but delivers another.

The Father was offering me the same committed relationship I had with a cigarette. However, his offer didn't have strings attached like Satan's did, leading to death. God's offer included security and assurance; he wanted to be my best friend, lord, and king.

I knew God was asking me to let him be my number one, my ride or die. I could envision my life totally devoted to him. Seeing what my life would look like if I let God replace the cigarette, I was scared.

This is something that the prophet Jonah can connect to. Reading Jonah's story, I got the clear message that if I didn't obey the Lord, I could get swallowed by a whale. I often get the message that compliance is better than disobedience, which is true, but the Lord has shown me that there is more insight to be gleaned from this short book, particularly for people who suffer from addictions.

God gave Jonah, a prophet of Israel, specific instructions. He had to travel to the "great city of Nineveh" and deliver the Lord's judgment. Jonah was familiar with this magnificent metropolis in the Assyrian territory. The Assyrians were preparing to unleash their devastation on Israel. They were not kind people, and Jonah was terrified because he knew he was the enemy in their eyes, just as they were in his.

Jonah had to decide whether to flee the battlefield or go into it to deliver God's punishment. What a conundrum. I was in the same situation—the Lord was urging me to give up smoking and put my faith in him. I wanted to, but I couldn't think of a time when I didn't rely on cigarettes to get by.

I knew powerful things lurked inside of me that needed to be brought into God's light, and the great city of myself was quite a mess. Some things stood out more prominently and vied for power over me. Certain thoughts and actions screamed loud for my attention: the addictions, the food, the need to control and manipulate, and the desire to be loved. Feelings of being unworthy, unlovable, unreachable. Thoughts that told me I wasn't good enough and I never would be. This was my battlefield, and God wanted me to call out the lies I believed and replace them with truth.

The terror I went through thinking about facing these things without my constant companion, a cigarette, left me feeling paralyzed—stuck and unable to move forward. I was tempted to think and adopt this lie: "I've always smoked; why quit now? Jesus will always love me and forgive me."

Fear can be viewed as Face-Everything-and-Rise or Forget-Everything-and-Run. Jonah chose the latter, as did I.

Jonah got up and went in the opposite direction to get away

from the Lord. There was no way he was going to Nineveh. That place was filled with his enemies. I often wonder, when Jonah envisioned himself going to Nineveh and proclaiming God's truth the first time he was commanded, did he get excited over the initial vision? But then, with the thought of accomplishing the vision, he became so overwhelmed with raw fear that he needed to run. I understand. Even though I could imagine myself living a Christ-centered life in my head, it terrified me to let go of the addiction to embrace my heavenly Father. *What if he disappoints me?*

Jonah's ability to recognize the Lord's voice indicates that the two of them had frequent conversations. Since I've read this story several times, it's easy for me to skim over the intricacies, yet doing so would be a mistake. This is an example of one of them. Jonah knew the Lord was speaking to him even if he chose to ignore it. Their connection is shown in this. Jonah was already acquainted with God. During their conversation, they exchanged words.

While Jonah and the Lord are in a relationship, it occurs to me that it only takes one step to start going in the opposite direction from the Lord. One step. It can happen without even being aware. At the first hint of working through the things God wants to shed his light on (a stronghold), as soon as we put an obstacle in the way of dealing with these, we take the first step away from the Lord.

As I thought about this, a picture formed in my mind. On one side was a messy pile of my thoughts and actions; on the other side, I was walking away. As I walked, I noticed a long string of spaghetti feeding my brain the same lies repeatedly. Standing between the lies and the truth was the Lord in the ready position, at the entrance of my Nineveh, when I got scared and fled because I didn't want to look at the years of hurt and abuse.

In my mind, the steps away at first were slow, but then they began to pick up momentum until they were quick, and soon they were sprinting to put distance between me, the problem, and God. I could see the Lord standing with the problem or issue, his hand outstretched, inviting me to go with him. I didn't have to face the hurt and pain alone.

Jonah's journey found him on the port of Joppa. He was desperate, alone, afraid, and looking for a way to escape. He did not want to go to Nineveh, he wanted to go as far as he could in the opposite direction. The Lord has suggested to me this simple fact: Jonah could have turned around at any time, but instead, he let his fear keep his footsteps quick.

The importance of the harbor was lost on Jonah. It was a fork in the road. He could either run from the Lord and go to Tarshish, head to Nineveh, or remain on the port of Joppa. The resemblance to substance dependency is glaring. Looking back, I realize there was a turning moment in my cigarette addiction when I felt I was no longer in control of my decision to stop. Similarly, there was no turning back after Jonah boarded the ship.

Like Jonah, I often missed the crossroads signs in the past, but not on that morning. I knew God was asking me to let him be my best friend. I was faced with a choice: Do I surrender my addiction and face the giants lying within? Do I continue to run, or do I stay on the port?

I could get comfortable on the port and blend in with the many others there, whom the Lord has asked to deal with something, maybe something from their past or a situation that is happening right now, but they don't. They choose not to because they are afraid, but they don't want to get on the ship and go out to the deep sea, so they camp on the river's edge and make a comfortable home there.

But not Jonah. No, he got on the ship. He made the choice to get on the ship and put as much distance between himself and the Lord as possible. He was not going to camp on the shoreline, and he was not going to Nineveh; he made up his mind that he was going west.

Jonah was sleeping in the bowels of the ship when the Lord flung the powerful wind, causing a violent storm. I don't like to think about this side of the Lord very often; when the storms of life come, I'm more apt to say, "This storm is from the devil." I am not saying that the Lord brings all the storms into my life because sometimes it is the forces of darkness, but I needed to understand that there are times when the Lord also brings them.

God showed me the key difference between him bringing a storm and when forces outside of him bring a storm. It boils down to this one thing: obedience. Am I being obedient to what God is asking me to do? Am I dealing with the things God is asking me to deal with? I once heard it said that delayed obedience is still disobedience, partial obedience is still disobedience, and revised obedience is still disobedience. My choice to obey or disobey the Lord has good and bad consequences.

I was quick to let the Holy Spirit transform me in most areas. My potty mouth disappeared instantly, but I wrestled daily with my cigarette addiction.

I longed for the external signs of my sinful life to be removed. Instead, God, in his kindness, showed me that cigarettes were the Band-Aid for the hurt I endured. The cover allowed me to hide my internal pain, like my fear of rejection, abandonment, or being loved, because I have believed the lie that I am unlovable for so long. For a long time, I had a driving need to control things or to manipulate situations because I feared setting healthy boundaries.

Sitting in my living room, contemplating what God was asking of me, I became painfully aware of my fear of bringing all my shortcomings and sins into the light of God's truth; I knew my heart was living on the port of Joppa. I didn't like to admit to fallibility in my life, but these lies are the ones that keep me disconnected from the vine. These fears and inward thoughts are transformational areas. My rejection has been transformed into acceptance in God's family. My fear of abandonment was replaced with assurance, even if my father and mother abandon me, the Lord will never leave me. The rest is chaff to be burnt up and tossed out. God has taught me courage is not the absence of pain, suffering, or fear; rather, a person can find strength in the face of pain and grief to move forward.

On that morning, I decided with God to quit smoking. Even though God was with me on the journey, I knew it would still be a challenge. A cigarette was such an intricate part of my day, I had smoked a pack of cigarettes a day for years and was dependent on them to get through my day. My life was centered around my addiction, and the tension of fighting a battle I would never win, but sitting cross-legged in my living room, something had shifted in my mind.

Instead of fighting the battle against my addiction, I needed to start surrendering it to God. I realized it was the only way I was ever going to be free from the death grip of the cigarette.

I started to pray and ask God to show me areas in my life where he wanted to be first instead of a cigarette. I asked him to help me break the habit and to become more dependent on him.

At first, I struggled with the idea of giving up the habit altogether, but as I sought guidance from God, I realized I could achieve this goal with him. I started to replace my cravings with activities that brought me closer to God, such as reading the Bible and praying.

I also looked for other activities to keep myself away from cigarettes.

I also became aware of my environment. Where did I like to smoke, and what food or drink did I like to smoke with? Was there a specific time of day I preferred a cigarette? I realized these things were triggers for my addiction, so I made a conscious effort to understand them. As I understood them, they lost their power over me.

As I continued to surrender my addiction to God, I began to see changes in my life. Not only was I free from this addiction, but I could see other areas of growth. I was starting to become more independent from cigarettes and could go for longer periods without needing to smoke. I was also becoming more connected to God and finding more joy and peace in my life.

The Lord gave me a mind shift; before I knew it, I was no longer thinking of smoking, and I went to a ladies' retreat weekend and never smoked while I was there. Once I returned home, I didn't start again. I practiced mindful meditation and relaxation techniques.

I am grateful for the journey and growth I experienced through the process. I learned that with God, I could overcome my addiction. He was always there to help me along the way.

The apostle Paul wrote in Galatians 5:1 (NIV), "It is for freedom that Christ has set us free." To live in the freedom I had been set free for, I needed to repent from thoughts and areas of my life that he was asking me to and allow the Holy Spirit to transform me, matching my inside to my outside. This took courage, and there was pain, but the Lord's promises are true and trustworthy. He was with me.

Gentle Challenge

Spend time with the Lord and ask him to search you to reveal anything that needs to be brought into God's light.

Reflection Questions

1. Is the Lord calling you to go to Nineveh to pronounce his judgment on an area of your life?

2. How do you see Jesus showing up in this area?

3. When you think of what truth God is revealing, what will your life look like after you have dealt with the truth?

Fear, Faith, and Freedom

Journal Your Thoughts Here

Pray with Me:

Dear heavenly Father

Thank you for showing me areas where I put other things in place of you. Please forgive me and take your rightful place as lord and king of my life. I ask that you be above all and that my life is fully surrendered to you. Help me to overcome fear to lay this area down.

In Jesus's name,

Amen.

Scripture Memory Verse

It is for freedom that Christ has set us free.

Galatians 5:1a NIV

Lights, Camera, Action!

"What is going on?"

My little heart worked overtime to figure out why the lights were off in the gymnasium.

"When are they going to turn on the lights?"

"Where is my teacher?"

The buzz of my classmates tried desperately to calm my dread. *This is by far the worst assembly I have ever attended. What was...*

The light suddenly flicked on at the front of the room. There. Standing before us was a young girl with long red braids secured in place with green bows. Freckles covered her nose and cheeks, and her eyes twinkled like diamonds. She wore the plainest green dress I'd ever seen, which covered her ankles. She clasped her straw-brimmed hat in one fell swoop as her eyes looked up. "If I must stay at this train station for the night, I could sleep on that branch right there. It looks sturdy enough to hold me."

Hearing her words and with the stage light on, my body relaxed, engulfed in what was happening onstage. My mind transported to another time and place as *Anne of Green Gables* came to life. My fears and worries fell away, even if for a moment. And in that moment, I fell in love.

Anne taught me about resilience, courage, and self-belief. She encouraged me to dream of a life where anything was possible if I dared to take the first step and never give up. After all, if Anne could sleep in a tree for a night and face the dark all by herself, I could do hard things too.

My love for make-believe had me seeking every opportunity to escape to a different world. I would often imagine I was the host of my favorite TV show, *Polka Dot Door*, in the privacy of my room. I loved Humpty, Dumpty, Marigold, and Bear. We would go on adventures to other places, and yes, sometimes the Polkaroo showed up to play with us. I found myself drawn deeper into my new world of make-believe.

A couple of weeks after we saw *Anne of Green Gables*, I was sitting at my little wooden desk. The teacher standing at the front of the classroom cleared her throat. "Class. Class. If I could have your attention for a few moments, I have an announcement."

My eyes and ears were paying close attention. I could hardly believe what she was saying. "Class, we are going to put on the play Snow White and the Seven Dwarfs, and if you would like to be in the play, you can audition for a part. Be sure to pick up the script on your way out."

As quick as the bell rang, I raced up to the front of the class to pick up a copy of the script and skipped out the door. I couldn't wait till I got home to start memorizing the lines. I was going to try out for Snow White. I would be perfect. Although my skin was a little darker than Snow White's, I still thought I was the best choice because of my dark brown, almost black hair cut into the perfect bob. I could tie a red ribbon in my hair like Snow White.

I rushed home and barreled in through the door. "Mom, guess what? There is going to be a play at school. *Snow White and the Seven Dwarfs*, and I am going to play Snow White."

"Did you get the part?" she yelled from the couch as I raced up the stairs to my bedroom.

I couldn't wait to start practicing the part of Snow White. "Not yet."

I emerged from my bedroom only to eat the whole weekend. Otherwise, I could be found reading the play to my friends Humpty, Dumpty, Marigold, and Bear. I gave them each a part to play and memorized their lines as well.

When it came time for the auditions, I was ready. I came prepared to conquer the stage. Not only did I memorize my lines, but the entire play. I mouthed the words while they were being spoken on the stage. The teacher saw this and was amazed that I knew every line in the play, and because of this I got cast. I didn't get the part of Snow White though, only the understudy.

My little soul held out hope because I knew even though I was the understudy, someone had to go on if something happened to Snow White or anyone else in the play, and it would be me. But alas, the moment never came. I stood to the side, mouthing everybody's lines, thinking, *What's wrong with me? Why aren't I good enough?* I thought of what to do next time to make them pick me, thinking I could somehow control it. Even as a young girl, my value and worth were tied to how I made people feel.

The disempowerment I felt from behind the scenes watered the seed in me to strive to be something great and reach perfection, because that is how you get accepted—codependent thinking at its finest. I learned the art of people-pleasing and mastered the art of faking it for another's approval.

Fast-forward a few years as I entered the fourth grade. I was extremely excited to start because the music teacher was going to be my teacher for the whole year. She was the best. I started attending the school the previous year during the middle of third grade, and she had welcomed me and made room for me in the choir after she busted me for smoking. She saw me. She truly saw the broken little girl I was and loved on me. She encouraged me with truth and tried to help my self-confidence.

Walking into the classroom, I noticed that the walls were

decorated with number cards portraying simple equations. The cursive alphabet was atop the chalkboard, boasting the words, "Welcome to Grade Four." Right underneath was this slogan: "Do to others as you would have them do to you—the Golden Rule."

The slogan spoke right to my heart and my head by reaffirming the lie that if I behaved a certain way, people would like me, and it heightened the lie even more by telling me that I could control people by how I treated them. If I wanted them to treat me well, then I needed to treat them well.

This misguided truth played a huge part in leading my life. It taught me how to be manipulative. If I wanted something, I learned how to act to receive what I wanted. Unfortunately, it didn't show me how to get the good stuff I craved—love, acceptance, and a place to belong.

On the school grounds, I became the defender. I always stood up for the underdog. If I saw someone picking on someone else, I was right there. I would stand between the two and fight for the one being picked on. The underdog became my new best friend until the next person came along who needed some protection.

In my mind, I was living out the Golden Rule. I desperately wanted somebody to stand up for me. To stand in the gap, take the hits, stop the abuse, and tell me everything was going to be okay. I wanted someone to protect me.

Years later, you can imagine my surprise when I learned the Golden Rule was directly from Scripture, and the Lord revealed the truth of this passage to me. By putting the passage into proper context, I saw it meant Jesus is teaching us how to respond when people attack, lie about, and persecute us. Not how to get attention.

The words Luke wrote have nothing to do with treating people well to be treated well. Jesus wants us to respond to negative treatment, not react. When we respond, we are normally calm, cool, and collected. Our response is thought-out and edifies the other person. When we react, we do so without thinking. The impulse within rises to the surface, and we act out of our emotions.

When we react, it can make the situation worse. Our emotions heighten, and we unintentionally escalate things. Our adversary, Satan, loves it when we do this. He loves any time he can cause our thinking to be out of alignment with the Word of God. He thrives when our relationships are broken because he can play with our confidence. Without a godly intervention, we never reach the Godfidence God wants. Confidence says I can do it. Godfidence says God will do it through me.

This understanding was so liberating. I didn't need to be perfect or control situations to make people like me. This allowed me to understand when someone chooses not to like or respect me, it has nothing to do with me but everything to do with them.

Jesus' teaching me the truth of the passage reaffirmed a new belief. I don't get my value from people or situations. I get my value from God. The one who created me equipped me with everything I would need to live this life. With this new mindset, I could see how I brought value into situations I was a part of.

We bring value to every relationship and experience we have, from the ordinary to the extraordinary. We can add to the value of others through encouraging words and affirming them, but their value is not dependent upon us, and ours is not dependent on them. The same is true for each situation you will ever face. You bring something significant to the table. No one else has what you have to offer.

God knew the right amount of strength I would need to battle addiction. He knew the mindset I would need to over-come abuses in my life. He knew the boldness I would need to proclaim his truth. He knew the hardship and suffering I would endure and gave me the tenacity to live this life. Before the foundations of the world were laid, God knew me. He had a purpose and plan for me. He knew exactly what I would need to live my best life with him.

The Lord has emboldened me enough to declare that I am a masterpiece created on purpose, with intentionality, to complete a mission for such a time as this. It took me many years of recovery and the peeling back of emotional layers to agree with the Word in Ephesians: "For we are God's masterpiece. He has created us anew in Christ Jesus, so we can do the good things he planned for us long ago (Ephesians 2:10 NLT).

God knows us intimately, and because we are his masterpiece, he has placed a piece of himself into each of our spirits. When we live knowing our value comes from God and understanding who he has created us to be, we can live in the freedom of becoming.

In Revelation 1:18 (NLT), Jesus says, "I am the living one. I died, but look—I am alive forever and ever! And I hold the keys of death and the grave." These two words, death and grave, have very different meanings. Death signifies the act of becoming. Jesus holds the keys to death, meaning the day, the time, the hour, right down to the second. Jesus is in control of our becoming all God created us to be.

Each day we die to ourselves, we are becoming. When we say no to the substance or toxic relationship, we step closer to becoming the person God created us to be. That transformation is possible because we choose to believe what God says about us.

Each day I choose to submit to the Father, I am released from the death and decay of my sinful nature and renewed in my mind and spirit.

Dying to self is a core concept in the Christian faith, yet it can sometimes feel abstract or difficult to grasp. At its heart, dying to self means surrendering our own desires, selfish ambitions, and sinful tendencies to God's will, allowing him to shape us into who he created us to be. It is a daily process of transformation—of becoming.

Letting Go of the Old Self

Jesus said, "If anyone would come after me, let him deny himself and take up his cross daily and follow me" (Luke 9:23 ESV). The cross was a symbol of death, meaning that following Christ requires a willingness to let go of anything that hinders our relationship with him—our pride, our unhealthy habits, our need for control, or anything that competes with God's place in our lives.

Becoming More Like Christ

Dying to self doesn't mean losing our identity; it means becoming who God originally designed us to be. Paul wrote, "I have been crucified with Christ. It is no longer I who live, but Christ who lives in me" (Galatians 2:20a ESV). When we surrender our will to God, his Spirit transforms us, replacing our old ways with his life-giving power.

The Daily Battle

Dying to self is not a onetime event—it's a daily decision. Every time we choose to forgive instead of holding a grudge, to trust instead of worry, to obey instead of rebel, we are participating in this process. As Paul said, "I die daily" (1 Corinthians 15:31 NASB), meaning that he continually set aside his own desires to follow Christ.

Freedom Through Surrender

At first, dying to self may sound like losing something. But in reality, it is gaining everything. Jesus said, "Whoever loses their life for me will find it" (Matthew 16:25 NIV). When we let go of our limited, self-focused way of living, we receive the fullness of God's purpose, joy, and peace.

The Power of Resurrection Life

Jesus's words in Revelation 1:18 remind us that he holds the keys of death and the grave. When we surrender to him, we are not left in a state of loss. We are raised to new life. Just as Jesus rose from the dead, we are renewed and empowered to live in victory over sin and brokenness.

What does this look like?

I choose to seek God daily. I offer control of my day. I believe God is going to do what he says he will. I embrace my reality. And I remember I am not alone. In other words, I choose a S.O.B.E.R. lifestyle.

Dying to self is not about losing who you are. It's about shedding the layers of sin, doubt, and fear that keep you from becoming all God intended. It is a daily surrender, but in that surrender, we find the greatest freedom. We find our super-power—Godfidence.

The apostle Paul says he runs the race to attain the perfection Jesus perfected him for. The day we say the big eternal yes to Jesus, God's vision for our lives is perfected because it will come to pass. We are told Jesus, who began a good work in us, will complete it. It will be finished. Paul didn't know all the plans God had for him, but as he faithfully did the next right thing, the transforming work of Christ accomplished what it set out to do.

When I was young, my grandpa kept a full key ring in the deep pockets of his pants. When he walked, I never knew if he had a pocket of coins or keys. I used to ask him all the time why he had so many keys. His answers always varied depending upon his mental state. If he was sober, it was short and to the point: "Because I need them." But if he was intoxicated, he gave different answers. The more drunk he was the funnier the answers got. His imagination was wild, but make no mistake, he knew each key's location and what it was for.

I'm sure Jesus holds a similar-size key ring for each soul his Father created. Not one person was created to be an understudy. Each person is created to shine. To take center stage and to elevate the name of Jesus.

Jesus tells us in Matthew 16:19 (NIV), "I will give you keys to the kingdom of heaven[.]" These keys are to invite people into the family through a relationship with him.

The Lord holds the keys to death, life, and our destiny. For those of us who've accepted Jesus as our personal Savior, he holds the key to understanding who we were created to be and how our lives will all come together.

His Word says he plans a future full of hope for us. No eye has seen, nor ear heard, nor mind imagined what God has prepared for those who love him.

We don't have to wait until we reach heaven to discover our destiny. We can live a life of expectancy here on earth as we become more and more like Jesus every day.

God is orchestrating everything in this world that has been broken so that it can be restored to its divine purpose. He wants to use us as his hands and feet to take the broken pieces and restore them to wholeness. He wants us to be bold, courageous, brave, and full of confidence in him.

When we choose God's way, he gives us the strength to walk into our destiny and live our highest calling.

Gentle Challenge

Spend time with the Lord, asking him to reveal areas where you like to get your value. Ask him to show you instead how to bring your value to those areas.

Reflection Questions

1. Is there a misguided truth you learned as a child that you need to rethink?

2. How will you rethink this to form God's truth in your thinking?

3. In what area of your life do you need to step out in Godfidence?

Journal Your Thoughts Here

Pray with Me:

Dear heavenly Father,

Today we cry out to you, Abba Father. Create within us a spirit of Godfidence. Help us to live with the expectation of adding value to situations instead of receiving value from them. Set us free to be dependent on you. In Jesus's name, we pray.

Amen.

Scripture Memory Verse

Love your enemies! Do good to them. Lend to them without expecting to be repaid. Then your reward from heaven will be very great, and you will truly be acting as children of the Most High, for he is kind to those who are unthankful and wicked. You must be compassionate, just as your Father is compassionate.

Luke 6:35–36 NLT

Chapter Four

Embracing My Identity

"Lord, you know I can't do that. I can't tell people that. Do you know what they will do?" I said as I tapped my thumb softly on the space bar.

Suddenly, the screen in front of me became a vulnerable space. There was nowhere to hide, and oh, how I wanted to. Desperately. How could I tell people all my story? To some, I would be looked at as a great overcomer. To others, I would look like someone who couldn't struggle with that because you're born this way, and it is not something you overcome but embrace. Yet, God asked me to write about a secret I have buried for years. I liked women.

Same-sex attraction—this subject is so taboo and misunderstood in our church culture. Satan has been having a field day, keeping many good Christian men and women trapped in a place they don't have to be because they feel they have nowhere to discuss this. Instead, we hide in shame and secret, even after overcoming it. This dirty little secret has held me captive for too long because the truth is that same-sex attraction doesn't define who I am. It never did, and it never will. I am an overcomer because of Jesus Christ.

It wasn't easy to come to terms with the inner battle I was fighting, an attraction that did not align with what I knew to be true. The struggle was real, and I was losing the battle until something changed within me. I began to discover my identity in Christ.

I know the confusion stemmed from words spoken to me as a child. The memory is as fresh in my mind as the day it happened.

I was eleven years old and asked to babysit. I arrived at the house thinking, "I hope the kids behave tonight." When I opened the kitchen door, the lady stood in a shiny red jumpsuit, stirring a pot on the stove, with one of her babes on her hip. She looked stunning. "Va va voom!" I exclaimed.

Her head turned toward me. "Are you gay?" She didn't wait for me to answer and continued with her task.

The question lingered in the air like thick smoke with nowhere to go while my little mind tried to process the question. Even though I felt I was advanced in my knowledge of sexuality because of sexual abuse, I wasn't prepared for such a question. I knew what it meant for a person to be gay. But was I gay?

I stifled a laugh. "No. I'm not gay." I'm unsure if she believed me, but this question came up a lot. I did think girls were pretty, but I also thought boys were handsome. I liked being friends with girls, but I also liked being friends with boys. Should I not tell people when they look good?

Her question confused me and stirred up my curiosity. Was that why I liked to climb trees and got along better with boys than girls? Or why I liked a good bike ride? Some of my favorite places to play were outside and building forts to hide in. My friends and I would explore all over, but did this mean I was gay?

I was overwhelmed with the thought of being something I wasn't, and if I was gay, what would my family say? I heard them talk, heard the insults hurled at people who were different. I didn't know what to do and felt helpless. So, I did what I learned to do since birth: stuff those questions and feelings deep into the cracks of my hurting heart and confused mind. I tried to counter people's negative comments with a good joke because it was easier to laugh than cry.

I kept my secret of confusion safely hidden until I had been married for seventeen years. I tried to keep my feelings from showing. I was determined never to tell someone they were pretty or looked good again because I didn't want anyone else to ask me about my sexuality.

We were getting ready to celebrate our seventeenth wedding anniversary, and Ken and I had this brilliant idea that we should try swinging. As we looked into the lifestyle, we discovered many bisexual women were involved in this community. I instantly felt a connection to the people in the community, even though I had not yet met one person. I no longer felt so alone in this area of my sexuality. Many women labeled themselves bi-curious, so that's what I did. I introduced myself to the whole world of swinging as bi-curious.

Entering the realm of swinging was like stepping into a different universe, where my inner fears were acknowledged and embraced. This lifestyle represented a whole new level of freedom, but at the same time, it also opened a realm of exploration and even confusion. The term "bi-curious" resonated with the unsettled pieces of my identity, and I resonated with others who bore the same label. This community was where I could be myself without fear of judgment or rejection. However, the initial excitement eventually faded as I questioned whether this lifestyle truly aligned with the values I held dear.

As our journey in the swinging lifestyle progressed, it invariably reflected a mirror on the unhealed parts of our relationship. This so-called newfound freedom became a glaring spotlight, illuminating an old wound that we had implicitly chosen to ignore, an extramarital affair from our early years of marriage. A trauma we thought was in the past, neatly tucked away, hidden behind the veil of time and denial, suddenly resurfaced with an intensity neither of us were prepared for. The lifestyle we had embraced, which promised liberation, opened Pandora's box, setting free the ghosts of past betrayals we could no longer ignore.

As the ghosts haunted our present, we found ourselves on the precipice of confronting the painful truth at the heart of our journey. The affair, a memory we'd tried to bury, was not just a betrayal but a desperate attempt on my part to quench the growing thoughts of lesbianism within me. I thought that by stepping outside the bounds of our marriage and seeking another man's affection, I could somehow suppress these feelings and bury them deep within. I was terrified of admitting to myself, let alone to my husband, that I was attracted to women. Yet, in grappling with the fallout of the affair, I began to confront the full spectrum of my identity and embarked on a grueling but necessary journey of understanding, acceptance, and, ultimately, healing.

Over the course of a transformative three weeks, we found ourselves ensnared in an intimate cocoon where time was lost and healing was found. Submerged in the ocean of our bedsheets, we embarked on a deep, soul-searching conversation that flowed like a peaceful stream, unearthing hidden truths and reconciling them with newfound understanding. We cried, we talked, we listened, and we grew. We discovered the bed was no longer just a place of rest but a sanctuary of healing, a battleground where we fought against our fears and insecurities, and a cradle where we nurtured our love and cultivated acceptance. In that surreal in between of sleep and wakefulness, we found strength in vulnerability, and in admitting my attraction to women, we found the courage to dismantle the facade we had crafted to hide our pain. This was the beginning of a healing process that taught us our love was not just about gender but about souls connecting, creating a bond stronger than any label could define.

Sitting in the bed, completely naked, I felt beautiful for the first time in my life. Not a superficial sense of beauty, but the real beauty that comes from within, the kind of beauty God designed when he created a man and a woman in the Garden of Eden. In these sacred moments, I felt like one of God's treasures to display his splendor and glory. Even though I was living far from God at that moment, if ever a masterpiece had feelings, I was feeling them.

Amid our healing and self-discovery, I started to distinguish between what constituted good sex and bad sex. Good sex, as I began to understand, was not solely about physical satisfaction but had a much deeper emotional and spiritual dimension. It was about intimacy, connection, understanding, and mutual respect. It was about holding each other's vulnerabilities with tenderness, embodying love in its purest form, and cherishing the sacredness of our shared experience. On the other hand, bad sex was superficial, lacking emotional depth and connection. It was about seeking temporary pleasure, a fleeting escape from the realities of life. This understanding transformed my perception, making me realize sex was not merely a physical act to be endured but a spiritual journey of love where two souls met, understood, and comforted each other.

This was the intimacy I craved. For so long, I wanted this but had no clue what it looked like or how to achieve it. But here we were, Ken and I, finally experiencing true intimacy. The kind of intimacy the apostle Paul describes in the love chapter of 1 Corinthians, both inside and outside of the bedroom.

Through prayer and reading the Word, my thoughts were cleansed, and my identity was secure in Jesus. It changed everything. Jesus viewed me as a beloved daughter, not an ugly, perverted, confused mess. That was the title thrown on me but not by my Father. Seeing how Jesus viewed me allowed me to like myself for the first time.

The love chapter, 1 Corinthians 13, is a profound discourse on the nature of love. The apostle Paul describes love as patient, kind, not envious or boastful, not proud or rude or self-seeking. He tells us love is not easily angered, keeps no record of wrongs, and does not delight in evil but rejoices with the truth. Paul explains that love always protects, trusts, hopes, and perseveres and never fails.

This passage, when applied in the context of our journey, brought a new understanding of our love. It helped us understand the depth and breadth of love God desires for us, a love not defined by labels but by the qualities it possesses. Our journey was starting to align with Paul's description of love, allowing us to see that our love was patient when we forgave each other, kind when we comforted each other, and enduring as we persevered.

Through their timeless wisdom, Paul's words presented a vision of love that transcends physical attraction and delves into the realm of the soul. It provided a framework for us to build a relationship not based on fleeting desires but on the solid foundation of mutual respect, understanding, and, most importantly, agape love—the highest form of love, the love that God has for us. This Scripture helped us see that our love for each other was not a mistake but a reflection of God's divine love for each of his creations.

I can see now how God was preparing me for what He would do in my life and marriage. It took many years for me to truly understand my identity. But coming to terms with who I am wasn't about denying something I wasn't—it was about turning to God and his Word to discover the truth about who I am.

As I continued toward self-discovery, the revelation of God's Word became my guiding light. Through the Word, I began to understand myself more profoundly, seeing my identity not through societal labels but through the truth of who God created me to be. God's Word, a mirror to my soul, reflected a deeply loved, cherished, and accepted woman. This revelation was not an overnight transformation but a gradual process of peeling back the layers of guilt, shame, and confusion. Through the divine wisdom of Scripture, I began to see myself as God did—a beloved daughter, not defined by my desires, but by my God-given identity. I was no longer lost in a sea of uncertainty; I had found my anchor in God's unfailing love and understanding. This was a crucial step in my journey toward self-acceptance and understanding, a metamorphosis directly linked to the teachings and promises in his Word.

Living without shame became a cornerstone in my journey toward self-acceptance. For years, I had been shackled by the heavy chains of guilt and self-condemnation, but the transformative power of God's love set me free. A beautiful verse in Romans 8:1 (ESV) says, "There is therefore now no condemnation for those who are in Christ Jesus." This verse became my mantra, my declaration of liberation from the stifling cage of shame that had imprisoned me. I learned to forgive myself, to accept my past, and to embrace the whole of me. Even recognizing my same-sex attraction was a ploy of our accuser, Satan, to cause confusion and strife, not because I was born that way. Instead of living in shame, I chose love—God's love for me, my love for others, and most importantly, my love for myself. This self-love is a form of respecting myself. This shift from shame to love was necessary for my healing journey. Only by shedding the shame could I truly experience the depth, height, and breadth of God's unfailing love. Embracing my identity in Christ, I could step out of the shadows of shame and into the radiant light of his unconditional love.

Love—God's love for you, your love for him, others, and yourself—is the key to stepping out of the shadows of shame and into the radiant light of his unconditional love.

Gentle Challenge

Take some time to reflect on your own journey of self-discovery and acceptance, allowing the transformative power of his love to free you from any chains of guilt or shame.

Reflection Questions

1. How has God's love shaped your understanding of who you are?

2. What confuses you about who you are in Christ?

3. Are you ready to embrace your identity in Christ and experience the depth, height, and breadth of God's unfailing love?

Fear, Faith, and Freedom

Journal Your Thoughts Here

Pray with Me:

Dear heavenly Father,

Thank you for not abandoning us in our struggles and confusion. You show us that our identity is not grounded in anything but our status as your beloved child. You've taught us that we are not defined by the things of the world but by your unending love for us. Heal us of any false identity that can consume us and replace it with the truth of our identity in Christ.

In Jesus's name, we pray.

Amen.

Scripture Memory Verse

So now there is no condemnation for those who belong to Christ Jesus.

Romans 8:1 NLT

Chapter Five

Nursing My Wounds

I sat staring at the pile of weed on my bedside table. Try as I might, I thought I would never be able to leave this relationship with my drug of choice. It welcomed me each day to escape the hurt and pain until it only added to my hurt and pain. And by this time, the cycle of addiction was well ingrained. I was consumed with chasing the feeling from my very first high. I could release all my cares and concerns with just a few puffs. Now, though, a few puffs were never enough, and I needed additional substances to reach a level of being comfortably numb.

The pile of weed on my table seemed to mock me. If it could talk, I imagine it would say, "You thought you were strong enough to handle me. You fell for it, hook, line, and sinker. I can't give you what you want. You knew that, yet you still came back to me. You always come back to me. You are mine. I'm the only one who can help you."

I just wanted the insanity to stop, but each day, the pattern repeated. Einstein says, "The definition of insanity is doing the same thing over and over and expecting a different result." This was my life. I would go to bed with the resolve that tomorrow would be different. When I got up in the morning, the self-talk went like this: *I am just going to have one beer and one joint to get over the hump of the morning, then I will have the rest of the day to busy myself with distractions.* A couple of hours later, after the high wore off, it was easy to justify the second joint and my fourth beer.

This morning was no exception. Sitting on the bed, I knew

I didn't want to die like this but didn't know how to stop the crazy. I exhaled discouragement and drank in liquid hope. I didn't want to live, but I didn't want to die. I was hopeless, and I felt powerless to change.

As I watched the smoke twirl up in the air, I was genuinely dead inside and wished to disappear like the smoke.

"Mom," my daughter hollered out to me as she entered the door for lunch, giving me cause to interrupt the discouraging thoughts. "There's a lady at the door for you."

"Tell her to come here," I yelled back from my bedroom, thinking it was a friend.

Turning around the corner, her head peeked into my room, and with a sternness, she said, "No. Mom, she can't come in, and you need to get up and go to the door." Her voice told me this was serious.

I pushed my bedside table to the side. I slowly got up, closed my bedroom door, and made my way down the dark hall. My stomach lurched as I sensed the anxiety of my daughter. *What the heck is going on?*

I opened the door. "Hello."

The blonde lady stood there with her clipboard in hand. "Are you Jennifer Turner?"

"Yes. Who are you?" I asked, although I already knew.

"My name is Violet[6], and I am from Family and Children's Services. May I come in?"

"No. You can't come in." I responded in the most sober voice I could muster.

"Do you know why I am here today?"

"No. I don't know why you're here." I knew, but I wasn't admitting to anything. These people could ruin your life. I know because I was a ward of the courts. I know the stink that comes from having a file opened with Family and Children's Services.

"Are you sure I can't come in to talk to you?"

I held my ground. "No. You cannot come in."

"Today at school, your youngest daughter reported your drug use and drinking. She said you have no food, and no one cares for her. She is afraid for her life. Are you sure I can't come in to discuss this?"

"No, you cannot come in. You can come back later when my husband is home, but you are not welcome in my home right now." I wanted to slam the door, but I knew it wouldn't get me anywhere.

"Okay," she said. "I will come back at 6:30 p.m."

"All right. See you later." I closed the door. My insides were shaking. Now, what was I going to do? The one thing no parent wants to have happen happened.

Later in the evening, Ken was home, and we sat across from the social worker after she did a tour of our home. She laid out all the accusations against me. I know Ken was listening, but all I heard were audio mumblings. I was in disbelief and shock. While my daughter was being truthful about the drugs and alcohol, the other accusations were baseless.

The social worker gave me one week to be out of our home and off to rehab, or they were going to take our children. It made absolutely no sense; they don't normally take a person's children if one parent is struggling with addiction and the other parent isn't. Ken was not a weed smoker nor a drinker. He worked full-time, paid our bills, and bought our food, of which there was plenty.

If the truth is known, my baby girl wanted her mom back; this was the only way she knew how to get her.

I spent five years running from God. Not knowing how to deal with the church hurt I was experiencing at the time, I left the church one Sunday and vowed never to return. I was mad as hell at God for allowing such horrible things to occur at our church. I didn't understand the invitation to suffer with Jesus. I fought it and, instead, suffered alone.

Going through the pain of losing so many loved ones in one year was unbearable. I was also experiencing attacks from people who said they cared for me. I was broken. I was done.

Ken's dad was one of the many passings. He went to bed one night and didn't wake in the morning. I watched my husband lean over the bed of my father-in-law, broken and bruised from all the things left unsaid, left undone. It was a vulnerable moment, and he wanted comfort. When he left the hospital, he reached for a cigarette for the first time in years. He was searching for comfort and didn't know the Lord intimately at the time.

Our lives changed overnight. We became homeowners with two cars and no sense of stability in our finances. It was a disaster. To make matters worse, a dear saint in our church family caught wind of Ken smoking, and she felt it her duty to inform us through a letter that Ken was going to hell. She felt it was her obligation to also inform us that, because of his decision, our children were not being cared for spiritually.

Ken put the letter down on the table and declared with no uncertain terms, "I and our children will not be going back to that church. You do what you want, but we won't be going." And he didn't, nor did our children. I was a district-licensed minister at the time and felt I had to stay.

The next six months of life in the church were hellish. It was a dark place to be, spiritually, mentally, emotionally, and phys-ically. The tension could be cut with a knife when you walked in the door. The spirit of gossip, slander, control, manipulation, and offense was high. The congregation was having difficulties, and I felt caught in the middle. I wanted to support my husband, and I wanted to follow the call of God on my life. I never thought I would have to choose. But here I was, and I didn't know where to turn. The elders in my denomination offered me no guidance. Even when I voiced my concerns to the one who had been selected to facilitate conversations of restoration, he made fun of me for voicing my concerns.

Brokenness fed my decision to leave the church. Without mincing any words, I cried out to God, "If this is what serving you is like, I'm good. I will pass if this is what being part of your family is like. No thanks. I would rather go back and live my childhood over again. At least my biological family never claimed to be people they weren't." The brokenness of the body of Christ dumbfounded me. What should be a place of love, acceptance, and a godly family was a place filled with hurt, distrust, and untruth.

I took back everything God had healed me from: smoking, drinking, drugging, and same-sex attraction, and why not throw a few more bricks in the wall? I was arrested for assault. I prostituted myself because I was showing God who was in control.

For the next five years, I nursed my wounds. I took them out carefully every day to examine them. I went over them with a fine-tooth comb. I pulled apart every conversation and every interaction, looking to justify my behavior.

I slipped right back into the victim mindset. It was easy. It fit like I was born for it. I was in my place of comfort and getting lost in the cycle of addiction. I knew where I was going. I had been there before, and I didn't care. I didn't see what Jesus offered me, the opportunity to be so intimate with him in my suffering.

Suffering with Jesus is one of the most privileged places to be invited. In our pain, he is with us. In the dark night of our souls, he comes to meet us. We will never lose heart if we can stand firm in his presence and let him take away all that is not from him. I missed it. But through the courage of a broken girl, my baby, he reached down to me and said, "Come, follow me." I thought it was too late, but here he was, offering me a place. I was scared and unsure, but I knew it was the only way out.

God is close to the brokenhearted, yet I felt like he was a million miles away. The journey back to him was not easy, but I knew it was the only way. He had a plan for my life, and through the darkness, he revealed himself in ways I could never imagine. And when I needed comfort, he would wrap his arms around me and tell me everything would be okay.

The evening after the social worker left, I went on Facebook, trying to forget the events of the day. I had no idea what I would do, and I didn't want to think about it. As I got lost in the scroll, up popped a chat box from an old acquaintance. I had met her twice before when our families got together for meals. I went to the ministry development center school with her husband to become a pastor, and we became friends. I never really knew her, but that night, she became a safe person. She asked a simple question, "Hi Jenn, how's it going?"

She had no idea of anything happening in my life. She and her husband had moved to the East Coast of Canada. They were an eighteen-hour drive away. So, I told her the good, the bad, the ugly. Mind you, there was not much good. I told her my dilemma of having to be out of my home within a week and the horror of trying to get a bed in a rehab facility, which was next to impossible.

Her reply caught me off guard. "You can come and stay with us for as long as you need." I was in shock. She was offering me a place to stay in their home until I got my life back on track, exactly what I needed.

My friends became an unexpected source of strength. They showed me love, kindness, acceptance, and patience. Words cannot express how God used them to save my life.

As I stood in the line, to go through security at the airport, tears streaming down my face, a whole host of questions screaming for attention: When would I be home? Would I be okay? Could I actually do this? I was walking into the unknown. I had just said goodbye to my husband and children, feeling afraid, and with the events of the week replaying in my mind, I needed this to work. I needed God to work. He was my only hope.

That whole week, I kept seeing the blonde-haired social worker sit across the table from me. In my mind, I could see her mouth moving, but the words I was hearing were not lining up with her facial movements, "One week, you have one week… or we will take your children. One week…take your children."

Standing there, broken, naked, vulnerable, and filled with shame, with a one-way ticket in hand, I was off to Prince Edward Island. No return date in sight, my only mission was to get sober. I had been drowning my anger, guilt, and shame with drugs and alcohol; I was exhausted and could not run anymore.

In the airport lineup in my hazy reality, God gave me a vision of Jesus cradling me in his arms, whispering into my ear, as my head nestled into the crook of his neck, that my time in the wilderness was finished. I knew I was going to be okay. My suffering was coming to an end; I was coming home. For the first time in a long time, I wept because of a great swell of hope from this vision of restoration and redemption. Jesus was giving me another chance.

Once my feet landed on Prince Edward Island, God began to reveal through the story of Gomer in the book of Hosea how he orchestrated the events of the past few weeks to bring me here. I saw myself in Gomer, a woman hedged in by her own despair and rebellion. Just as Hosea pursued Gomer, I felt myself being pursued by God in my darkest moments. The walls that seemed to close around me, much like they did for Gomer, were not there to imprison me but rather to guide me back to the heart of my heavenly Father. In this vulnerable, hedged-in place, I discovered a love so profound my mistakes or rebellion could not outdo it. In fact, it was at these crossroads of my life that his love shone the brightest, drawing me back into his redeeming grace and unwavering mercy.

In the depths of my despair, I was reminded of a potent message from God to Hosea about Gomer. The Lord had said, "I will hedge her in with a thorn bush. I will strip everything from her. I will turn her valley of trouble into a gateway of hope" (Hosea 2:15, my paraphrase). This passage came to me not as a threat but as a promise of redemption. Much like Gomer, my life had turned into a thorny wilderness; everything I held dear had been stripped away. I was in my valley of trouble, but God's promise gave me hope. The thorny hedge was not there to harm me but to protect me from straying further away.

The stripping away of all I held dear forced me to confront my own rebellion and reevaluate what truly mattered. In the valley, I found not only trouble but how my troubles were also a gateway to hope for my life and others. His words gave me the strength to endure the pain of working through the overwhelming emotions, knowing my hardship was not a punishment but a path leading me back to his love, grace, and hope.

As I dwelt in my valley of trouble, enveloped in darkness and despair, I reached a critical juncture. I had to make a choice to either continue nursing my wounds and wallow in self-pity or confront my pain and seek healing from the only source who could truly mend my broken spirit—God. As painful and scary as it was, I made the decision to stop pointing fingers at God for the wounds life had inflicted on me. Instead, I chose to lay bare my pain before him, to expose my wounds so he might heal them. This confrontation was a pivotal turning point in my journey back to God. It marked the initiation of my dialogue with him, a conversation that began with my silent screams, echoed in the depths of my despair, but gradually transformed into whispered prayers and, ultimately, into a harmonious symphony of trust and surrender.

Gentle Challenge

The thorny wilderness of your life is not punishment but a path leading you back to his love, grace, and hope. What is the thorny wilderness you face?

Reflection Questions

1. How does the profound realization that you are being pursued by God transform your perspective on suffering and redemption?

2. When faced with the choice to either wallow in self-pity or confront the pain and seek healing, what are the key factors that influence your decision?

3. How does a dialogue with God through pain and suffering shape your journey?

Fear, Faith, and Freedom

Journal Your Thoughts Here

Pray with Me:

Dear heavenly Father,

Guide us through the thorny wilderness of our lives and lead us back to your love, grace, and hope. Help us turn away from blame and resentment and instead embrace your healing touch. Give us the courage to confront our pain, to navigate our valley of trouble, and to walk faithfully through the gateway of hope.

In Jesus's name, we pray.

Amen.

Scripture Memory Verse

> But then I will win her back once again. I will lead her into the desert and speak tenderly to her there. I will return her vineyards to her and transform the Valley of Trouble into a gateway of hope. She will give herself to me there, as she did long ago when she was young, when I freed her from her captivity in Egypt.
>
> Hosea 2:14-15 NLT

Chapter Six

Abiding Life

Lying on the flat hospital gurney, I stared at the ceiling, trying to count the little black flecks on the tile. Anything to take my mind off what was happening. The doctor's words swirled in the back of my mind. "Tubal pregnancy... Baby in the fallopian tube... We need to terminate, or you will die... You are almost twelve weeks. There is no time to wait. The fallopian tube could rupture."

The nurse sounded more like Charlie Brown's teacher than the encouraging voice she was trying to be. "Wah-wah. Wah, wah, be okay. Wah—wah, all right, Mrs. Turner?"

The lights went black.

I woke up in the maternity unit on the fourth floor, alone. The room was full but had an eerie silence. I desperately wanted a smoke. My heart ached as I saw the bassinet by the window, empty. A few hours ago, I was going to become a mother, but suddenly I wasn't.

The nurse came in to check my IV, blood pressure, and incision. The fatal cut that had removed my baby. The child I cried for and longed for. I had known the heartbreak of miscarriage before—three times, in fact—but this felt different. Even though I could do nothing for my precious baby, I still had to sign the papers for the termination. How could I? My body and my mind were equally desperate for comfort.

"Is it possible for me to go for a smoke?" Tears trickled silently down my cheeks.

The nurse's caring eyes looked deep into my eyes, and for a moment, I felt seen. Softly she said, "Aw, you do speak." She smiled.

My spirit sensed all the words she couldn't say. I managed a crooked smile back.

"If you can get up, you can go for a smoke. That's the rule around here," she said as she covered my body back up after carefully checking the operation site.

Once she left the room, I was determined to get out of bed and make the fifty-foot walk down the corridor to the smoking room.

I shuffled my body slowly down the hallway, holding my incision to ensure it stayed in place. If it didn't move, it didn't feel too bad. I stopped after a few steps to steady myself, grabbing the handrail. *Smokers heal quicker because of the sheer determination to get to this room for some real comfort.*

The stale smell of cigarettes greeted me as I opened the door to a small room with enough seating for four. Still supporting my incision with one hand, I gently lowered my body to sit in the orange-covered chair with the other. My movements were slow. My body hurt as much as my heart.

I smiled at the lady sitting across from me. She was a bigger lady with short, dark brown hair. She had the most amazing smile. I thought, "It's either talking to her or thinking about what happened."

"Hi. I'm Jenn."

"Hi, Jenn. I'm Vi."

The rest is history. Vi was twenty years older than me, and we became instant best friends. She mothered me through one of the darkest periods of my life—mourning the loss of one of my babies. We were a gift sent to each other from the Lord.

From the moment we were in the hospital smoking room, we developed a friendship spanning nearly thirty years. Over the course of our friendship, there were times we lost touch with each other, but as soon as we found one another, we would pick up right where we left off without skipping a beat. God always seemed to allow us to run into each other when we needed a friend to lean on during a specific season of life.

One thing that united us but also separated us was our faith. We are both believers, but we are from different theological backgrounds. I am not talking about different denominations but about different camps altogether. I am a from a holiness denomination, and she was from the Jehovah's Witnesses. At times, we had some very heated discussions about our faith stances. We both asked questions of the other, causing us to stop and think.

During one discussion, we discussed our faith in Jesus Christ, and because of our different camps, she made a comment trying to discredit my faith.

After the initial feelings of anger at her trying to invalidate my relationship and my love for Christ, I set to work on the Bible study I was preparing for our ladies' group. While preparing, I was reminded and encouraged through the Word that as a disciple of Christ, I needed to stand firm in the salvation and grace I had received.

If this had happened when I was younger, I would have handled it differently. I would have tried to argue with her. I might have had some words for her for not respecting my faith, and more than likely, I wouldn't have been willing to forgive her. This makes me thankful that I am a branch on the Vine and that I have been pruned in the area of reacting instead of responding.

In the Gospel of John, Jesus teaches that he is the vine; the Father is the gardener, and the disciples, including you and I, are the branches. When I first read this, I thought the branches being thrown into the fire were things in my life that were un-Christlike in nature, but when I put this passage in context and really looked at what it says, there is more to it.

When Jesus declares, "I am the true Vine," he is stating there is no other one to hope in or believe in; no one can save your soul (John 15:1). His Father is the gardener and is the one who prunes and tends to the garden.

Jesus cuts off every branch that doesn't produce fruit. Some things in our lives do not align with God's Word and must go. Some things will be cut off and discarded, but some will be transformed into lasting fruit, the kind of fruit that builds our character.

Transformation doesn't happen overnight. It takes intentional work every day. I have had to learn how to keep track of my heart. I disciplined myself to take time to ask questions and then sit with the answers, even when those answers are uncomfortable. I asked, "How is my heart? What is currently motivating me to do the things in my life? Does my life look a little like Judas's, like I am close to Christ, but my heart is far from him?"

Jesus taught the disciples the truth about his Father and his kingdom for three years. How to live in it. What it looks like. Things they will see in it. How to enter it, and the things they will do there. These truths have been pruning and preparing them for greater fruitfulness in the kingdom.

I often wonder about Judas and his experience with Jesus. Judas traveled and lived with Christ for three years. It appeared to everyone, even the other eleven, that he believed in Christ and was wholeheartedly living for him and with him, but Christ knew the moment Satan entered him, and Judas's heart became hardened. Judas allowed greed and selfishness to be his motivators, so he was cut off from the Vine. He shows no fruit or transformation in his heart after encountering Christ personally.

Not only did Jesus spend every day with these eleven men standing before him, teaching them, correcting them, and loving them, but he also witnessed their heart transformation. He watched them grow as they soaked in his teaching. Their eyes opened to areas in their lives needing change. Jesus taught them that pruning and transformation didn't stop with the knowledge they already had. It didn't stop the day after he was arrested. It didn't stop the day after he was crucified. It didn't stop after he rose to life, and it didn't stop after he ascended to heaven. It doesn't stop even after he sends the Comforter. It doesn't stop...ever. They were being prepared for a life of eternity in heaven.

I, too, am being groomed for eternity. This revelation explained so much about situations in my life and in my relationship with my friend Vi. We loved each other but kept bumping up over our different faith camps. We were divided. I knew in my spirit that I was right. She assured me of the same. It felt like we were on the proverbial hamster wheel of conversation. I know I didn't handle those beginning faith-based conversations very well. I wanted to prove I was right, as did she. In the end, we would decide that because of our differences, we should probably not talk about faith anymore. However, how do you not talk about your relationship with Jesus when you talk about your life? We both continued to respond the same way until we decided to take a break.

We both failed to realize God was pruning us. He taught us to respond with holy love by repeatedly bringing us to the same situation. The old way of doing things had to not only go away, but it needed to be transformed so a new way could develop, one that is like Christ.

I am so thankful for God's grace and pruning as he brings me to these situations so I can learn to handle them in a grace-filled, God-honoring way. I couldn't prune or transform myself. I needed a power much greater than I to do it.

At best, I could bring about a temporary solution, but the authentic transformation is an internal surrender. I had to surrender my brokenness to the Lord so he could heal and transform what was damaged. God promised to meet me in my brokenness and restore me. For God's promise to be fulfilled in my life, I had to surrender all the pieces. To be able to do this, I had to learn to seek him. By doing this, I was training myself to remain in the Vine by spending time with him daily, reading his Word to cleanse my thoughts, and having conversations with him where I was listening more than talking.

The longer I abided in the Vine, the more the Holy Spirit revealed to me the brokenness lurking within. It was more than a damaged spirit or low self-esteem; it was the image of God that was broken within. Each time someone called me a name or put me down, they spoke against the image God had designed for me. Each time someone violated me, they violated the image of God within. People ruined what God designed. The brokenness within caused me to lash out and exhibit many unhealthy behaviors.

This final evening of teaching the disciples as they were accustomed, Jesus was driving the point that their relationship with each other was valuable. They needed each other; the journey wasn't meant to be walked alone. The serving wasn't meant to be done alone. A friend of mine often says, "No man is an island," which is so true. We were created to have relationships with a need to be loved and love others.

Jesus also knew that in this life, there would be personality clashes. Not all people will get along 100 percent of the time, but as branches of the Vine and a world reading us like a Bible, there had better be something different about how we handle conflict and love each other.

Love encompasses so much more than forgiveness. How are we serving each other? Are we encouraging one another? Are we bearing the burdens of one another? Are we praying for one another? Are we spending time with each other? If we see our brother or sister in need, are we helping?

I told you earlier about my friend Vi. I had a choice to forgive or hold a grudge. She sent me an email saying she was sorry for saying those things and attacking me and wanted to know if I could forgive her. A younger me would not have resisted the temptation, and I would have chosen to hold on to the unforgiveness. But not today. I am not that person anymore. I have been transformed in that area. So, instead of reacting, I sought wisdom to respond with grace and the love of Christ.

It took me awhile to learn the cycle of my thinking, but it started with this thought: Why can't I move past this? Or why does this keep happening to me? The Lord challenged me to think about what he was doing in my life. Then the lights came on—God is pruning me. After that change, different questions surfaced: Is there a different way I could handle this situation that is more honoring to the Lord? Have I sought the Lord for his guidance?

Gentle Challenge

Spend time with the Lord and ask him to search your heart to reveal areas where you need to learn to respond with holy love.

Reflection Questions

1. What is an area you seem to keep coming up against?

2. How do you see Jesus showing up in this area?

3. When you think of the situation you keep coming up against, is this something that is transformable, or does it need to be thrown in the fire?

Journal Your Thoughts Here

Pray with Me:

Dear heavenly Father,

Thank you for not leaving us as you found us and for seeing us as wonderful creations. We know you are pruning us for the plans you have for our lives, even when it hurts. Thank you for being our safe space.

In Jesus's name, we pray.

Amen.

Scripture Memory Verse

He cuts off every branch of mine that doesn't produce fruit, and he prunes the branches that do bear fruit so they will produce even more.

John 15:2 (NLT)

Chapter Seven

Unconditional Love

I pushed the window open, letting the warm night air drift in as I gazed into the darkness. My small bag lay by my feet, packed and ready. How dare he hit me, all because of a button.

Earlier that evening, I sat at the dining room table, tangled in thread and frustration, trying to sew that wretched button onto a piece of fabric. My fingers fumbled, the thread twisted and slipped—first too tight, then too loose. When I missed, his ruler came down, sharp and cold, biting into my arm. I clenched my teeth, fighting back tears, struggling through each botched stitch, each fresh slap of wood against my skin.

In the quiet of my room, I hugged my knees, staring at my hastily-packed bag. "I can't stay," I whispered. "Anywhere is better than here."

I slung the bag over my shoulder and climbed out the window, feeling the rough coolness of the TV antenna as I shimmied down, careful not to slip on the metal rungs. The night sky stretched above, scattered with stars, while the hum of crickets and the flicker of fireflies filled the air around me, soft and indifferent.

As I walked, my footsteps found a steady rhythm, but my thoughts kept tripping over themselves, tangled with words I'd heard so often I could barely distinguish them from my own. Jennifer, you're worthless. *Jennifer, you're just like your dad. Jennifer, you'll never amount to anything.* I tried to push them away, but the phrases returned, circling back like echoes that refused to die. The words sliced deeper than any ruler could, leaving wounds no amount of silence could soothe.

I tried tuning the words out with the little ditty I had been taught at school: "Sticks and stones may break my bones, but names will never hurt me." The more I countered, the harder they attacked. This ditty was a lie because these names hurt and were seared into my brain.

My hands fumbled to get the cigarette out of the package. *Who does he think he is? Doesn't he know he isn't my father? Did he not get the memo?* Charging down the street, I flicked my lighter. *He wasn't there the day I was born, yet he walks into our house and acts like he owns it.*

And that's when I heard the mysterious voice. "Jennifer, you're going to be okay." I knew it wasn't mine because it was deep and throaty, and I was an eleven-year-old girl with a squeak. This wasn't the first time I had heard the voice. I never questioned it. I struggled to believe it most times, but it always seemed to show up at the right time and always spoke so calmly to me. The softness of the voice reassured me and encouraged me. I had begun to look forward to hearing it, especially on days like today.

I reached my hiding spot—a dusty basement in an old apartment building. Nestled at the bottom of the stairs was a sagging leather couch, my fortress of solitude. I'd discovered it one rainy afternoon when an old woman had invited me inside to wait out the storm. Now, it was mine. Here, beneath the flickering basement light, I'd retreat with a cigarette in hand, letting the smoke curl around me, hoping it might somehow shield me from everything beyond.

"Why doesn't she stop him?" I muttered, my voice barely a whisper. "Doesn't she care?"

As I sunk into the worn leather of the sofa, the scent of old tobacco clung to the fabric, providing comfort. I was alone in my little world, a solitary figure in the dim, echoing stairwell. This was my sanctuary, my fortress of solitude. Its walls were lined with a profound sadness. I felt unloved, unwanted, and invisible to the world beyond these stairs. The sounds of laughter and life seeped through the cracks of families in their apartments, feeling like echoes from another universe, a world from which I was excluded. I pulled my knees to my chest, my cigarette dangling forgotten between my fingers, as I wrapped myself deeper into the cocoon of my brokenness.

The pain rolled down my cheeks, finding its way to the sides of my mouth, leaving a salty residue on my lips. *What does my mother see in that creep anyway?* I was so angry with her for bringing him home. *How could she? Doesn't she care about the marks he was leaving on me? Doesn't she love me enough to make it stop?*

He slung the word "b*tch" at me like a cheap, worn-out nickname. It was used as a tool, a weapon to degrade and diminish me, to cement my sense of worthlessness. It was like an ugly sweater forcibly thrown onto me, an unwanted branding I was expected to wear with passive acceptance. But each time it was thrust upon me, it served to stoke the fires of resentment. Was I more than a derogatory label or an insult casually tossed around?

"Jennifer, you're going to be okay." The calmness of the deep voice reassured me. A deep sob escaped my lips as I reached around to snuff out the last remnants of my cigarette in the ashtray. The white smoke twirled in the beams of light, invading the darkness. My body rocked with the sound of the words in my head: You're going to be okay. The rhythm lulled me to a place of calm.

I rustled from the lull. I had no idea what time it was, but I knew I needed to summon my courage to go home. I wanted to stay in the basement. Hide from the pain. A sigh escaped my lips as I reached for a fresh cigarette. With my friend securely in my hand, I rose from the worn leather sofa, my heart pounding against my rib cage. With each step I took toward the outside door, I knew I was returning to face the familiar chaos at home.

I desperately wanted different. I wanted a home I would be safe in. A family to love me. I was tired of feeling unwanted, like a piece of yesterday's garbage left for the trash and used like a common shovel.

Feeling unwanted was a consuming drain, a constant, unending ache. It seeped into my soul and tinged every moment with sadness. It was an emotional weariness going beyond physical fatigue, washing over me with a sense of being a ghost in my own life, unseen and unnoticed. It was fraught with sharp pangs of isolation. I stood on the outside, peering through a window at a world where I didn't belong. Each moment, each interaction, each glance from another human being became a confirmation of my insignificance. This yearning for acceptance and love gnawed at me, eroding my spirit until all that remained was a hollowness. It was an unbearable pain begging for change, a shift in the narrative, a hope for a tomorrow where I was no longer invisible but seen, valued, and loved.

A few short years later, after a major move to a new city, I found my way out. I went to my guidance counselor at school and told him about the abuse at home. I was removed from my house and became a crown ward in the foster care system, where I would age out at eighteen. Life wasn't perfect, but it was good. I settled into a foster home with other girls. I was safe.

Leaving the school on a sunny November afternoon, the air was crisp as I started for home, but my feet took a detour as I listened to the crunching golden leaves. The sun was too nice, and besides, what cool kid at fourteen doesn't want to hang out on the street corner with their friends? I was a cool kid or tried to portray that I was. We hung at a large wooden gazebo on the corner of our main street, which offered protection from the rains for those waiting for the bus. It also made for a great place to hang out, smoke cigarettes, and avoid getting caught.

As we hung out, talked, and joked around, we didn't realize the sun was going down and the moon was coming out. The night air settled in, bringing a chill to our bodies.

One car came through the intersection, hitting the other, causing a loud crash. As car parts flew over the road, the stores emptied out. Everyone within earshot wanted to see what the loud bang was, and I soon found myself in a swarm of people.

The smell of suede caused my head to turn, and there he was, a blond, handsome hunk who'd come out of the pool hall. He had his hair tucked behind his ears. His lip curled as he watched the event until our eyes met.

Without missing a beat, I said, "Can I wear your coat, please? It looks awfully warm."

"Sure," he said, taking it off and so graciously putting it on me. "What's your name?"

His smile captivated me as I answered him, "Jenn. What's yours?"

"Kenny." His grin widened.

"Thanks for letting me wear your coat. It smells really good." I wanted to die as soon as the words came out of my mouth. *He must think I am a dork. Who says that? "It smells good."*

I smiled back at him, wanting to crawl into the garbage can beside the gazebo. I quickly turned my attention to the commotion on the street and watched for a few more minutes. Thankfully, nobody was hurt.

Kenny shyly said, "Hey, if I walk you home, you can wear my coat, and you won't be cold."

"Sure. That would be nice." I pointed to the direction of the other end of the street and said, "I live down by the 7-Eleven."

"Me too," he said, and we began to walk home.

My quirky remarks were soon forgotten as we got to my house. We talked nonstop. Our conversation was easy. It felt like we had known each other our whole lives, even though it didn't make a bit of sense to me.

"Can I have your phone number?"

I rattled off the seven digits and floated inside.

———

Many years later, in my early forties, sitting in a circle of my peers during a ministry assessment, I had to share my testimony of God's transforming work. While I was sharing, the Lord, who is so gracious and kind, gave me the words to describe Ken's love for me. I had never verbalized them before but knew it to be true. Ken is the greatest example of unconditional love in my life. He is the only one who has ever loved me like Jesus. Seems what I had been searching for my whole life God positioned beside me.

This epiphany brought me to a deeper understanding of God's love for me. Ken and I have been through horrible experiences. I made some horrible choices. Some men would have gone running, but not Ken. And believe me, I tried to push him away so many times because he "deserved better." I always felt he could do better, have better, and be more if he cut me loose. He saw something different, though. He saw a treasure when I saw a piece of garbage. The saying is true: one man's trash is another man's treasure. He saw a potential in me I never could have seen. He pushed me to be the best version of myself, and his love has continued to carry me through my darkest days. I still saw myself as the worthless piece of trash left out for curbside pickup, but in this moment, I felt God's love wash over me profoundly. He solidified in me my adoption as his daughter. I knew I was an heir in the kingdom, and I was home.

Sitting in the chair, the tears of joy flowed as I had this full-blown revelation of God's unconditional love for me too.

There was nothing I could do to make God love me more, and nothing would make him love me less. His love is his love with no strings. He doesn't love us based on our behavior but rather because he is the essence of love.

"But God showed his great love for us by sending Christ to die for us while we were still sinners" (Romans 5:8 NLT).

I love this Scripture verse because it reveals God's heart toward us. God isn't expecting perfection, nor is he expecting good behavior. It says that while we were still sinners, Christ died for us. There was no expectation of holiness when I came to him. I put the expectation on myself. I was convinced I needed to clean myself up before God would accept me. This is not true. Christ accepts us bruised, broken, and wounded.

We are given a new identity in the name of Jesus. We are made righteous, called beloved, given authority, and blessed beyond measure.

The power of our name in Christ is great and mighty! Through this beautiful relationship with Jesus, we can go from broken to redeemed, from sinner to saint, and unrighteousness to righteousness.

This love of God is unending and ever present and changes us from the inside out. We can never earn God's love, but we can receive it. This alone brings freedom.

Gentle Challenge

Take a moment today and celebrate the goodness of God's love for you. Reflect on the power of your name in Christ and how it transforms you into an heir, beloved, righteous, and blessed beyond measure. Allow the grace of Jesus to wash over you as you receive his unconditional love.

Reflection Questions

1. In what ways have you experienced the unconditional love of God in your own life, and how has this shaped your self-perception?

2. How has embracing your identity in Christ transformed your relationships, choices, and approach to life's challenges?

3. What practical steps can you take to continually remind yourself of your worth and the power of your name in Christ, particularly during challenging times?

Fear, Faith, and Freedom

Journal Your Thoughts Here

Pray with Me:

Dear heavenly Father

Thank you for creating us so fearfully and wonderfully. Your workmanship is a marvel. We bow before you with adoration, giving you the glory for the mighty things you are doing in our lives. You lead us down the best pathway for our lives, and as we go, we discover who we are in you. Let us always see ourselves and others as you do, as masterpieces.

In Jesus's name, we pray.

Amen.

Scripture Memory Verse

> But God showed his great love for us by sending Christ
> to die for us while we were still sinners.
>
> Romans 5:8 NLT

Unplugging the Vacuum of Self-Sabotage

The darkness of the room brought comfort to my saddened heart. The hurt was overwhelming. There was no rhyme or reason for this pain. In fact, it was the opposite of what I thought I should be feeling.

I had just started a new job as an assistant manager at a restaurant, training youth in crisis with the law. It was a unique training program that taught them life skills like budgeting, CPR, and first aid. We poured into them as they learned kitchen skills and customer service. As far as jobs went, this was the best job I had ever had. I was using my life experiences with my pastoral education to help foster an environment of acceptance and learning.

As I pushed open the door from the restaurant, I could sense the familiarity of the emotions settling in. The over-whelming intensity of this darkness was not a new feeling. It gently wrapped itself around me like a suffocating hug and reminded me of the moments I had spent locked in my room as a teenager, feeling hopeless and lost.

As I made my way home, the day waned and morphed into a monotonous blur. A known heaviness started to seep into my existence. The vibrancy of the restaurant and the youthful energy that had stimulated my spirit during the day started to feel like a distant memory. The laughter and smiles of my staff, the sizzling sounds of the kitchen, the orders being yelled all turned into a background hum, a muffled symphony of sounds that I couldn't connect with anymore. The enthusiasm I had started my day with, my purpose to help these youth, seemed to have dissolved into a bottomless abyss of despair.

I never knew when the darkness would come to make my day an uphill battle against an engulfing abyss and debilitating emptiness. When it did strike, it would grow within me, threatening to swallow my essence. As I crawled into bed, it was evident to my husband and me that the insidious onslaught of depression had crept in, veiling my world in shades of gray.

As the veil blanketed my world, time bent and warped around me, stretching moments into hours and hours into days. The simple act of getting out of bed became an insurmountable task, akin to scaling a mountain without gear. My limbs felt heavy, as though anchored to the mattress, refusing to heed my mental commands. The hollow echo of my own breath seemed to fill the room, amplifying the silence as I lay motionless, the chasm between my body and mind deepening. The comfort of my bed, once my sanctuary, now felt like a cold, lifeless prison. The room that had been my private oasis was now a symbol of my isolation, housing my listless body and somber spirit. Two full days passed in this state, each moment tinged with a relentless melancholy that seemed woven into the fabric of my existence, making every thought and movement a monumental struggle.

On the dawn of the third day, a faint glimmer of hope sparked within me. Even though the daunting specter of despair still lingered, I felt a subtle shift. The immovable mountain I'd been scaling seemed a tad less intimidating. I could feel my limbs stir, a slow and hesitant response, like a dormant plant experiencing its first touch of spring after a long, harsh winter. I felt a slight detachment from the bed that had become my prison, a tiny fragment of willpower pushing against the relentless gravity of my depression. It was faint, fragile, almost fleeting, yet undeniably present. As I gradually slid my feet over the side of the bed and felt the cool touch of the floor beneath, it was like stepping onto an unknown terrain. The strength of this single act surprised me, piercing through the veil of gray. It was a small victory, a tiny rebellion against the oppressive darkness.

A whisper of resilience, my soul's way of saying, "I'm still here. I'm still fighting."

I didn't know what was wrong. As far as I could tell, nothing was wrong with me. I wasn't sick. I didn't have a headache. My kids weren't sick. My husband wasn't sick, but I sat in a vacuum of sadness.

The sorrow seemed to suck me into a black hole with no way out. I couldn't see two feet in front of me. All I could muster was to take my days minute by minute. It seemed like such a menial task when compared with the great achievements we were making with the youth in our program. But here I was, completely lost and alone.

Why did this dark cloud suddenly descend upon me? Hadn't I been doing everything right? Wasn't I using my gifts and talents to help others? Why, then, did I feel so empty inside?

I sat down on my couch, staring into the room's darkness. My thoughts rolled in like a freight train. *Do you remember when you quit this job at the local factory? Do you remember when you stopped working at the mall? That was a job you really loved but didn't stick it out. Why do you do this to yourself? Why do you always give up?*

Tears streamed down my face as I remembered all the times I had given up on myself and others. I was reminded of the times when I let fear and doubt take control, when I stopped believing in my own abilities and potential. Times I listened to lies spoken over me. And now, here I was, facing the consequences of my own actions.

The memory of buying a beautiful ornament at a flea market came to mind. I hadn't thought about that ornament in years.

As if on a movie reel, the day unfurled in my mind's eye. Warm sunlight filtered through the rows of trinkets and curios at the flea market. The air buzzed with the hum of excited chatter and the hawking of vendors. Each booth was a treasure trove piled high with relics of the past and curiosities from lands unknown. My heart pounded with a thrill of anticipation as I meandered through the labyrinth of stalls. Then, amidst the clutter, my eyes fell upon an ornate trinket that seemed to call out to me. A beautiful piece, infused with such detail and craftsmanship that it was impossible to ignore. A hurricane glass topper lay horizontally on deep-mahogany wooden pegs that housed the most stunning flower arrangement with candles to match on both sides. The vibrant peach and brown colors complemented each other. It was exquisite.

The moment I held it in my hands, I felt a connection, an inexplicable bond that seemed to echo some forgotten fragment of my soul. It was an encounter that felt significant, a moment frozen in time that brought with it a sense of calm in the eye of my personal storm. But looking at the price of $49.99, I thought there was no way I could spend that much money on an ornament.

Ken saw me admiring it and asked, "Do you like it, Jenn?"

"I do. I love the colors, and I think it would look really nice on our coffee table," I said with a smile from ear to ear.

"We'll take it," he said to the lady behind the booth.

I was flabbergasted as the lady started to wrap it up. My insides were giddy, and I went home like a child who had just come from the candy store.

Once at home, I displayed it on our coffee table and couldn't wait to light the candles. And just as I envisioned, the beauty added to the living room. I wanted to save lighting the candles for a special occasion because it was too pretty to melt yet. I wanted to savor the beauty.

Later, my parents came for a visit, and when my mom said how much she liked it, I couldn't help but give it to her. She didn't ask for it. She didn't even say she wanted one. She said,

"I like that. It's really pretty." That was all it took to be over-whelmed with guilt that I had something pretty and my mom didn't.

Purchasing something truly special, something you've yearned for, can be a profoundly spiritual experience. It's not just about having a new item in your possession; it's about the emotional journey, the anticipation, the deep-rooted desire that is finally realized. It's like a small manifestation of your dreams into reality, a testament to your hard work and perseverance. It's a tangible token of self-love, reminding you that you are worthy of delight and luxury.

As I reached for a tissue, it hit me—I was sabotaging myself. I was making the choice to stay home because I didn't feel worthy enough to have a job like this. Just like I gave away every nice thing I owned, I did it because I didn't feel I should have a good job or nice things. The words spoken to me as a child rung inside my head. "You are nothing and will amount to nothing when you're older." I was making it happen. These were my choices. No one else was choosing for me.

Amidst all the pain and regret, a small glimmer of hope appeared. Instead of wallowing in self-pity and berating myself for past mistakes, I listened when a small voice inside me whispered, "You are meant for more."

I couldn't ignore the voice. Words of hope reminded me of my purpose and potential. It reminded me that my past doesn't have to define my future; I have the power to make different choices and create a better path for myself.

I stood up, wiped away the tears, and decided to stop giving up on myself. To stop letting fear and self-doubt dictate my actions. And most importantly, to start believing in myself.

As I returned to work the next day, I felt lighter and more determined than ever before. I was excited to continue pouring into the youth in our program, but this time, with a renewed sense of purpose and self-worth. Because even though my journey has been difficult and filled with mistakes, it has also taught me valuable lessons and brought me to where I am today. And for that, I am grateful.

The struggle against self-sabotage is a quiet and often unseen battle. The silent whisper of doubt echoes in our hearts just as we are about to take a leap of faith. The unseen claw reaches to grab us and hooks its ugly chains to entangle us, keeping us from reaching our divine potential. Within us is an unshakeable spirit, a force of life more powerful than any fleeting thought or emotion. Overcoming self-sabotage is not just about breaking free from self-imposed limitations; it is about embracing the wholeness, the completeness, and the divine perfection that is our true nature.

From this moment onward, I became aware when my choices were self-sabotage and when they weren't. I chose to listen to the inner voice of courage and love instead. Whenever fear and doubt tried to creep in, I reminded myself I was meant for more and my journey was far from over. With this newfound determination, I finally said confidently, "Watch me soar."

In the Gospel of John, Jesus asked the man sitting by the pool of Bethesda, "Would you like to get well?" It seems like such a simple question, yet it is packed with power. The question implies there is something we must do to get well. It's not enough to desire or wish for wellness; we must act and make the choice to get well. Self-sabotage often comes from a place of fear—fear of failure, fear of success, or fear of change.

Jesus knew the man's story of being ill for thirty-eight years when he asked him about his desire to get well. He knew the man had become accustomed to his illness, which had become a part of his identity and way of life. But Jesus also knew that true healing requires us to let go of our past and embrace the present. To take responsibility for our choices and make an intentional effort toward wellness.

In the same way, we must be willing to leave behind our self-sabotaging habits and embrace a new way of thinking and living. We must be willing to let go of the limiting beliefs that hold us back and step into our true potential.

The man sitting by the gate responded to Jesus by saying, "I can't, sir," the sick man said, "for I have no one to put me into the pool when the water bubbles up. Someone else always gets there ahead of me." (John 5:7) The man responded from a victim mindset.

Victim mindset is a common theme among those who struggle with self-sabotage. It's the belief that our circumstances are out of our control and we have no power to change them. But Jesus didn't let the man stay in his victimhood. Instead, he offered him a solution. "Get up, pick up your mat, and walk."

With those words, Jesus invited the man to take ownership of his situation and make a choice for healing. And when the man did as Jesus said, he was miraculously healed.

We, too, have the power to choose healing and transformation in our lives. We can choose to let go of self-sabotage and step into our divine potential, embracing the fullness of who we are meant to be. It may not be easy, but it is possible.

I invite you to ask yourself, "Would I like to get well?" With courage and determination, I hope you respond as the man by the pool did: "Yes, I choose to get well." By choosing self-love over self-sabotage and embracing a life of wholeness and abundance, you will manifest your dreams into reality and live out your true purpose confidently and gracefully. The journey may not be easy, but it will be worth it. Let's take the first step together toward a life filled with joy, growth, and endless possibilities. So don't just dream big. Make it happen because you are meant for more. And I am here cheering you on every step of the way.

Take a deep breath, let go of all doubts and fears, and choose to believe in yourself. When you choose love over fear, miracles happen. And you're worthy of every miracle meant for you. Rise and embrace your true potential in Christ with open arms. The journey will be long, but the rewards are immeasurable. By moving forward, one step at a time, your life is filled with love, purpose, and abundance. And always remember you are meant for more. Never settle for good when God has promised you the best. Keep shining your light.

By choosing to listen to the still, small voice of God, you will find courage and love and take a stand against fear. When you choose to get well, the chains of self-sabotage break and you will walk into your true potential.

Gentle Challenge

For the next seven days, choose one area in your life where you experience self-sabotage. This could be in your relationships, career, health, or personal growth. Each day, consciously choose to do one thing that contradicts this self-limiting behavior. It could be as simple as choosing a positive affirmation over a negative thought, saying yes to an opportunity you would typically avoid out of fear, or seeking help when you'd usually try to do it all alone. Remember, it's not about perfection but progress. Embrace the journey, and know that with each small step, you are moving closer to your true and highest self.

Reflection Questions

1. What limiting beliefs am I holding onto that are preventing me from achieving my fullest potential?

2. In what areas of my life am I allowing fear to dictate my actions and decisions?

3. What can I do today to step out of my comfort zone and move toward my true, highest self?

Fear, Faith, and Freedom

Journal Your Thoughts Here

Pray with Me:

Dear heavenly Father,

We surrender our fears, our doubts, and our limitations to you. We trust in your divine plan for us, and we choose to walk this journey with faith and perseverance. We are ready. We are willing. We are capable because of your work in us.

In Jesus's name, we pray.

Amen.

Scripture Memory Verse

And God will generously provide all you need. Then you will always have everything you need and plenty left over to share with others.

2 Corinthians 9:8 NLT

Chapter Nine

The Leadership Staff

As the airplane touched down on the hot Cuban tarmac, the smell of burning rubber invaded my senses. *This is why I don't like to fly. The landing stinks. Literally.*

My heart pounded with a mix of excitement and nervous anticipation as I struggled to get my carry-on down from the overhead compartment. *These aisles must have been designed by a skinny person, for a skinny person.* My apple-shaped body was having trouble getting in the awkward position needed to extend my tiny T-Rex arms to take my luggage down without it falling on my head. Determination paid off, and I was able to assume the position to win the luggage battle, and no one was hurt in the process.

The hot sun greeted me as I descended the plane with my suitcase securely in hand. *This is it—the place I've been hearing of for years. What is God going to do?*

I completely forgot the burnt rubber smell as I scanned the most beautiful blue sky. There wasn't a single cloud in sight. The warm breeze kissed my exposed skin, daring me to trade in my warm winter clothes from Atlantic Canada for summer attire. I had heard so many amazing stories of the Holy Spirit showing up and doing miraculous signs and wonders, changing many people's lives drastically in this very place. What was I going to see? Would I experience something supernatural? My insides were giddy with anticipation.

As we made our way to the resort, my heart burst with excitement and adrenaline. My soul was thirsting for a deeper connection with God, and I believed this trip would be a turning point in my spiritual journey. *I am ready to open my heart and receive whatever blessings God has in store for me.*

As we arrived at the resort, we were greeted with warm smiles and tropical drinks. The vibrant colors and lively music instantly lifted our spirits, and we couldn't help but dance along to the beat. *This is what living in the moment feels like.* Surrounded by fellow believers, each of us knew this trip would be a time of spiritual renewal and growth.

Over the next few days, I immersed myself in the vibrant Cuban culture and connected with God on a deeper level through prayer, worship, and fellowship with other believers. God's presence was so tangible in this beautiful place. I saw the beauty of God's creation with fresh eyes as I saw things I had only ever seen in documentaries on TV. I was in awe.

During the evening services, the little cement church was full to capacity. The team of thirty was always given prime seating at the front of the sanctuary. We arrived an hour before we were due to begin, and people were already there. As more people gathered, more people worshipped. Each of us came with different gifts, and we used them. Eventually, there was a full worship band, Scripture readers, prayer leaders, dancers, and singers. When the Spirit leads worship, your mind, body, and spirit are fully engaged.

Our leader preached with passion, conviction, and transformative power. His messages were anointed from the throne of heaven. Scripture was served like a king's buffet. Each delicate morsel had value and gave life.

However, it was the prayer that changed me. Those who were praying had the ability to see things while they were talking with the Father. The Spirit was showing them things in the spiritual realm. Things being revealed were setting people free from emotional pain, limitations, addictions, and so many other problems. Seeing the transformation in people's lives was a true testament to the power of God.

I desperately wanted to go forward for prayer. If God wanted to give me something, I wanted to receive it and have nothing held back. But this stabbing voice of condemnation kept telling me, "You're going to look like a fool if you go up there and God doesn't have anything for you. Then, everyone will know you are nothing but a fake and a phony." It was the same old condemning dialogue, but then the inner warrior began to emerge. *Did you come all this way to sit in the pew or to experience everything God has for you?* Despite the fear, I stepped out to make my way to the front of the little Cuban church.

As the pastor prayed over me, he saw a tight-wrapped black cloth surround me. The cloth was trying to suffocate me. Later, the pastor explained to me that the cloth was symbolic of the lies and negative thoughts that had been holding me back from fully experiencing God's love and power in my life. Right then and there the pastor rebuked the cloth and told it to leave. I felt a release, a sense of freedom and lightness.

Later, in the quiet of my room, before turning in for the night, I grabbed my journal and began to write. "Lord, what does the black cloth signify?" As I poured out my heart on the pages, I could feel God's presence surrounding me. In my spirit, I sensed one word, "distrust."

It was true. Trust had been standing off in the distance while I tried to rebuild my relationship with God. I knew I needed God in my life but trusting him was a different story. I thought he had let me down. I thought he couldn't be trusted because the church treated me so poorly.

"God, I want to trust you, but you let me down big time. What if you do it again?"

Then God, in his great kindness, impressed upon me, "Do you remember when I brought you through this trial? Do you remember when I provided for you here? Do you remember when I did this and this and this?"

His kindness undid me as he gently opened my eyes to see all the different times he had showed up. "Oh, Father, I'm so sorry for not trusting you. I can clearly see you are trustworthy. You are constantly changing my faith in your faithfulness. Thank you." I was holding on to misplaced distrust. The truth is God is always trustworthy, but people will let us down whether they mean to or not. I was still letting a wounded view of the Father direct my relationship with him. With grace and the compassion of a father, he received my doubts and fears as I surrendered them. As the tears flowed silently down my face, I fell asleep in the sweet peace of Jesus.

The next morning, I was enraptured by our devotional. The leader spoke about Jesus on the Mount of Transfiguration. He was transfigured before John, James, and Peter. His face shone like the sun. "Moses and Elijah appeared and began talking with Jesus" (Matthew 17:3 NLT).

When Jesus went up the hill of transfiguration, he didn't take all twelve disciples with him. He only took Peter, James, and John. Our teacher pulled out this truth: not everyone goes up the mountain at the same time. There is an appointed time for each of us to go up the mountain of the Lord to experience intimacy like these three disciples did.

During the climax of the service, the pastor asked if we would like to experience the transformation. With anticipation and faith, we nodded our heads. We flocked to the front of the small sanctuary where the leaders stood by to pray over us. As we waited for our turn to receive prayer, we laid hands on those who were being prayed for and came into agreement in the spirit of what was being spoken over them. The worship leader sang a spontaneous song. As we sang and prayed, the presence of God became so thick in the room that it was tangible.

Finally, it was my turn to be prayed over. Standing in the

presence of the Lord, my body completely at rest, my arms in front of me with my hands open, palms up. *Lord, I surrender myself completely to you. Transform me, renew me, make me more like you.* As the leaders prayed, I could feel a warm sensation spread throughout my body. It was as if every cell in my being was being filled with God's love and light. Tears streamed down my face as I experienced an overwhelming sense of peace and joy.

The pastor cupped his hand over my head and, with his other, held one of my hands. "Father, thank you for your servant. She is willing. Use her." As his words fell over me, the love of God spread through my body, and suddenly, everything around me faded away. All I could hear were the pastor's words. "God is giving you a staff of leadership. You don't need to run; you don't need to prove yourself. God has set you apart, and whom he sets apart for himself, he sets apart. You simply need to accept the staff of leadership and walk in the authority you have been given." I received the stamp of the Lord and his ultimate approval. Not by my own merit, just the opposite. God's stamp is not something we can earn; it is given, but we must receive it.

Moses struggled to receive the Lord's stamp of approval and his place within the kingdom. He needed to grow into it, even at eighty years old. He had to learn to trust God and let go of his own insecurities.

Just like Moses, I, too, needed to learn to trust in God's love and power. I had been holding on to my doubts and fears, allowing them to hold me back from walking in the authority God had given me. But through this powerful encounter with God, I was reminded that it is not about what we can do or how much we can prove ourselves but simply about trusting in God and walking in the authority he has already given us. It is about accepting his stamp of approval over our lives and surrendering ourselves completely to him.

From that day on, my relationship with God took on a whole new level of intimacy and trust. I no longer held on to my doubts and fears, but instead, I surrendered them to God and allowed him to transform me into the person he had created me to be. I learned true trust comes from a deep understanding of God's love and faithfulness, and when we let go of our own insecurities and fully rely on him, we can walk in the fullness of his power and authority. So now, every time I see a black cloth, it serves as a reminder to trust in God's love and plan for my life, knowing that he is always faithful and trustworthy.

Trusting in God may not always come easily or naturally, especially if we have experienced hurt or disappointment from others in the past. But through surrendering our doubts and fears to him, allowing him to transform us, and fully relying on his love and faithfulness, we can experience a deeper level of intimacy with God and be bold as we walk with him. So, let us always remember to trust in him, for he is the one who will never let us down.

Trust God's faithfulness and watch as he continues to amaze you with his love and provision. The journey may not always be easy, but it will always be worth it when we are walking hand in hand with our faithful Father. Let go of misplaced distrust and allow God to lead you up the mountain where you can experience true intimacy with him like never before.

Gentle Challenge

This challenge might seem daunting at first, but remember, the goal is not about perfection but progression. I challenge you to surrender your doubts, fears, and insecurities to God daily for the next thirty days. Start each day by declaring, "Lord, I surrender my fears and doubts to you. I trust in your love and faithfulness." See how this small act of faith can transform your life and bring you into closer intimacy with God. Remember, it is in surrendering that we truly find ourselves and experience the fullness of his love. Are you ready to embark on this transformative journey?

Reflection Questions

1. Reflecting on your own journey, what specific fears or doubts are you now willing to surrender to God in pursuit of this transformative path?

2. How might your life change if you were to deeply trust in God's love and faithfulness, walking confidently in the authority he has given you?

3. As we progress into this thirty-day challenge, what steps will you take to ensure that this act of surrendering becomes a continuous part of your daily routine, beyond the challenge period?

Fear, Faith, and Freedom

Journal Your Thoughts Here

Pray with Me:

Dear heavenly Father,

We bow before you today, humbled and in awe of your love and faithfulness. We thank you for the transformative power of your grace and the authority you have given us to live freely in your kingdom. As we embark on this thirty-day journey, we surrender all our fears, doubts, and insecurities to you, trusting in your everlasting love and faithfulness.

In Jesus's name, we pray.

Amen.

Scripture Memory Verse

Then the LORD asked him, 'What is that in your hand?'
'A shepherd's staff,' Moses replied.

Exodus 4:2 NLT

Chapter Ten

All Out or All In

"When you're in Cuba, you're going to have to decide whether you're all out or all in." *What did God mean by that? I mean, where else could I go? And who other than the Father has the words of life? All in? Wasn't I all in since my first trip to Cuba?* The Lord's words baffled me. For weeks before my second mission trip to Cuba, the Lord's words twirled in my mind like a ribbon floating through the air. *What could he mean—all out or all in?* At times, with my curiosity building, I thought I would burst with anticipation.

These Cuban trips were becoming very popular. People wanted to go not only to see what God was doing but also to be a part of it. Shortly after coming back from my first trip, I had my interview for my district minister's license, and while sitting around the table with nine ordained elders in my denomination, each one asked questions as they felt led. There was no way to prepare for the interview because the questions were as random as the ministers sitting on the board. When the interview was finished, one of the ladies said, "I think I need to go to Cuba because you're different. God did something powerful in you there."

The evidence of God moving was in the people, as each one came back transformed into a more emboldened version of themselves. We all had "Godfidence." Godfidence is the assurance that we can't, but God can. So, I was baffled by God's words, but the time had finally come. I was going to find out what they meant. I would be with a group of Jesus-loving people to learn to serve God in ways I had only practiced in school. I was going to preach with a translator for the first time. This was going to be a whole new experience, and I was scared but excited.

As soon as we landed in Cuba, the journey to the hotel unraveled like a dizzying Technicolor dream. Our vintage yellow bus, with its faded paint and rattling windows, cut through the vibrant Cuban landscape, a collage of emerald-green fields under azure skies. The bumpy, uneven roads jostled us, each pothole an insistent reminder of the worn-yet-resilient spirit of the land. As we traveled, the scent of burnt sugar cane became a constant companion, sweetly cloying and oddly comforting. It mingled with the occasional sea breeze wafting in through the open windows, a heady cocktail that was both foreign and familiar. Outside, the intense tropical sun painted everything in a golden, dreamlike hue, starkly contrasting the icy winter we had left behind.

The pale, egg-blue cement walls of the sanctuary greeted us as we walked in the door. There were four slat windows on either side of the sanctuary, allowing air to flow or people to see and hear. For extra air circulation, portable fans hung from the ceiling close to the outlets so they could be plugged in. The benches were made of two-by-fours and then painted dark chestnut brown. There were no padded seats, and yet the folks would gather for hours with no complaints, only thankfulness for what they had. Their gratitude opened the door to a joy I had never seen before but wanted.

The services were unlike anything I had ever experienced. The Cuban congregation's passionate worship echoed through the walls as if the very building itself were alive with praise. Hands raised in surrender, voices lifted to heaven, they worshipped without restraint or hesitation. It was contagious, and soon, our entire team joined in, caught up in the powerful presence of God that permeated the sanctuary. We sang in Spanish and danced joyfully, our hearts bursting with love for the God who brought us here.

During one of the services, an elderly lady who remembered me from the first visit came up after the service and handed me a decorative hand towel she had handsewn. Her tight hug and tender heart caused my eyes to well up as I humbly accepted her precious gift.

During one of the services, our leader said these words: "Some of you who are here are going to have to decide if you are all out or all in." Instantly, my spiritual ears perked up. This message was for me. I was about to learn some great truths.

"Lord, I'm here. I'm open. I'm listening and ready to receive." Then nothing.

Even though I knew this message was for me and I took so many notes, I didn't receive the revelation that would stop me in my tracks and make me ponder for hours. The kind of revelation I was expecting didn't come.

The worship team made their way to the front of the small church, and they invited us to stand. I stood to join my voice to the mighty chorus of praise. With my hands lifted and eyes closed, the music faded into the background, and it was just me and the Lord.

"Father, thank you for loving me so much, even when you didn't have to. You know all the days of my life, and yet you still choose to love me. You tell us we can come to you with all our questions. You never tire of us coming to you. Today, Father, I am confused. You said I would have to decide whether I was all out or all in during this trip to Cuba. I know you meant for me to learn something during this service. Which I did, but I was expecting more. Was I expecting too much?"

"Jennifer, you have given me everything that hurt, caused you pain, or made you cry. You have given me all the sadness, the anger, and the addictions. You haven't held any of these things back, but now it's time to decide: Are you going to give me all the things you are good at? Are you going to give me all the things you're talented at? Are you going to give back to me all the gifts I have given you? I don't want only the broken parts, but all the parts. When you surrender all, I will show you what I will do in your life, but first, you must decide: Are you all out or all in?"

Now, my tracks were stopped. My feet stuck. It made sense then, the question. My thoughts had all culminated in that moment.

Bowing my head in surrender, with tears streaming down my face. "Yes, Lord. I am all in. All for you."

And with that simple yet profound decision, a journey of surrender leading to a life of holy boldness ensued. I had to let go of the things I held dear to my heart. The accomplishments I made. The talents I had. All surrendered to a powerful God. In God's hands, these gifts and talents grew deeper. They became more profound. I chose to no longer hold back any part of myself. To fully embrace all he had given me and use it for his glory because I was all in.

One of my favorite disciples is Peter. Peter was flawed and lived an emboldened life. He was always the first one out of the boat. Whether it was to walk on the water or to throw off his cloak and jump in the water to swim to shore to meet his resurrected Jesus, he lived a life of total abandonment for God. He was the one who denied Christ three times, but even knowing this, Jesus still chose him to be one of his disciples.

I don't always get it right. I sometimes speak out of turn. I sometimes want to shout Jesus from the rooftops, and other times, my voice barely squeaks. Jesus never turned Peter away, and because of that, I am assured he will never turn me away. And if you happen to identify like this too, well, there is hope for you too.

Peter's boldness and passion were things God used for his kingdom. He just needed to surrender it all. God will use our surrendered passions and boldness as well. We just need to be all in, fully surrendered to him. Letting go of the things that hold us back and holding onto him with both hands, ready and willing for whatever he asks of us.

In our journey with God, we often hold back parts of ourselves, thinking they're not good enough. But God wants us to give it all. To be willing to surrender everything, our strengths and our weaknesses, for his purpose. He wants us to live boldly, without fear or hesitation, because we know he is always with us.

Allowing this head knowledge to become heart knowledge gave me deep assurance that God was always with me, and it changed my perspective drastically. Psalm 32:8 (NLT) says, "I will guide you along the best pathway for your life. I will advise you and watch over you." If this is true, why did I spend so much of my time worrying about things I couldn't control when I could be trusting the One who did?

When Peter stepped out of the boat to walk toward Jesus on the water, his entire perspective shifted. The familiar security of the boat vanished, along with the comforting view of its interior. Suddenly, his feet found themselves on the uncertain surface of the water, requiring him to adjust to this new and unfamiliar sensation. The absence of solid ground beneath him must have felt peculiar, as he relied solely on his faith in Jesus. He was free. Totally unencumbered.

Peter lived in the freedom he was set free for, and there is a different view there. When you live your life for God like you have nothing to lose, you gain everything. I am not talking about material things; I am talking about taking risks for God. Not only do you get to see miracles happen, but you also get to be part of those miracles. You find out that you are part of something so much bigger than yourself. You get to discover your true purpose and live it out with boldness.

So let us be all in, surrendering everything we have to God.

Let's not hold back our talents, gifts, or passions but use them for his glory. And as we do, may we live boldly, knowing God is always with us, guiding us along the best pathway for our lives. And in doing so, may we experience a life of freedom, purpose, and holy boldness. So, my dear friend, are you all out or all in? The choice is yours. Choose wisely.

Gentle Challenge

Take a moment to really ponder: In what areas of your life are you still holding back from God? Is it your career, your relationships, or perhaps it's your dreams? Whatever it may be, consider the freedom that surrender can bring.

Reflection Questions

1. What specific aspects of your life do you feel most challenged to surrender to God, and why do you think you hold onto them?

2. Can you identify a time when you stepped out of your "boat," your comfort zone, for God? What did this experience teach you about trust and faith?

3. How can you live more boldly for God in your daily life? What practical steps can you take toward living a life of full surrender and holy boldness?

Journal Your Thoughts Here

Pray with Me:

Dear heavenly Father,

We come before you today with hearts yearning for your guidance and wisdom. We acknowledge our weaknesses, our hesitations, and the areas of our lives we've been holding back from your loving hands. Help us remember that in surrendering to you, we are stepping into the vast ocean of your grace and love. Dear Lord, like Peter, we want to step out of our boats and onto the waters of faith. Give us the courage to trust you, even when the storms of life threaten to overwhelm us. Help us to live boldly for you, using our talents and gifts for your glory. May we always remember that when we choose you, we gain everything.

In Jesus's name, we pray.

Amen.

Scripture Memory Verse

The LORD says, 'I will guide you along the best pathway for your life. I will advise you and watch over you.'

Psalm 32:8 NLT

Chapter Eleven

The Canvas Train: A Modern-Day Parable

Bathed in the soft glow of sun-drenched aisles, I found myself wandering aimlessly through the maze of a quaint, old-town craft store, my soul humming with the silent melodies of countless stories paintbrushes could narrate on blank canvases. It always surprised me what people could make from what appeared to be a few scraps of this, a couple of snips of this, and voilà—a beautiful centerpiece for the kitchen table.

One of my favorite aisles was the needlework on plastic canvas one. I loved taking small pieces of plastic and transforming them into usable products. The store had some of the projects completed and put on display for all to see. I had always been amazed by the intricate designs and how something as simple as plastic mesh could be transformed into a delicate piece of art. It was like watching magic unfold before me.

My eyes fell upon the most adorable train engine and caboose. Its rich, vibrant reds and blues drew me in. *Oh, this would be adorable on our son Sam's dresser.* In my vision, I saw his Dr. Seuss books all lined up in between. He will love it. I picked up the kit and began to look at everything that came in the bag. Everything was there; I wouldn't need to buy anything else. When I flipped the bag over, my heart sank. The price was nowhere in my budget. *Why did crafting have to be so expensive?* I thought as I slipped the kit back on the hook. Disappointed, I went home with an empty cart.

Imagine my surprise when, only a few weeks later, I was sitting at a friend's dining room table, thumbing through an Avon catalog. There it was. The exact kit for half the cost. *Are you kidding me right now?* My friend noticed the wild look in my eyes and asked me if I was okay.

"I'm fine." But my mind was racing with thoughts of how much money I would save when I ordered the kit.

Each morning, I would rush to the mailbox only to be faced with bills and things I didn't want. Yet, I was not disheartened because I knew it was coming. The anticipation built within me a sense of joy and excitement. My vision of what our son's dresser could look like was going to come true.

Two weeks of waiting felt like an eternity. When I opened the mailbox to see the package there, I quickly took it out, locked up the mailbox, and skipped back to my apartment unit.

I took it out of the package right away and read the instructions. It was a large piece of paper with a template of the plastic canvas for cutting it out. This looked easy enough.

The apartment is quiet; you should go smoke that joint before Sam gets up. Getting up, I went to the bathroom. I believed the lie that what I did behind closed doors was okay because no one could see it; I wasn't hurting anyone.

Once finished, I returned to the couch and started cutting the canvas. It went well for the first couple of pieces. It didn't take a genius to cut up two squares and down ten. No big deal. Then, it got a little more challenging. *Wait. Was that up ten, over two, up three, over six? I thought you were up for the challenge.* I had to cut some of the pieces two or three times, but I kept telling myself everybody makes mistakes, right?

Maybe, Jenn, you should take a break from cutting the canvas and try putting some of the yarn on it. You probably just need to give your eyes a break. Go smoke another joint, and then try the yarn.

I didn't realize there were a few different shades of red in the kit, so I grabbed the first one and started. After I had sewn on a few pieces, I took a little break to admire my handiwork, and that's when I realized I had used the wrong shade of red. My inner dialogue started as I ripped the stitches out to do it over again. *Jennifer, what is wrong with you? You can't even get the shade of red right? Maybe you're not high enough. You should probably go back to the bathroom to smoke another joint.* This pattern went on for quite awhile until one day, I just put it away. I always meant to go back, but never found the time.

Over the years, I would see the unfinished pieces in my craft tin, and when I did, I was reminded of my failure. I always seemed to start things and not finish; this was just another example of my failed attempts. When I saw my unfinished work, I would ignore it, think about something else, and move on. I don't know why I held onto it for so long, but something wouldn't let me get rid of it.

When I was a new Christian and sober, I was invited to a baby shower for a little boy, and while I was thinking about what gift to give, my mind went to this train. I felt it was a perfect time to finish it, and it would be a special gift. But first, I needed to speak with Sam.

"Sam, can you come to the living room, please?" I hollered loud enough for him to hear me over his video games.

A moment later, Sam appeared. "Yeah, Mom?"

"Hey, so I was invited to a baby shower for a little boy. Do you remember the train I started making for you when you were like two?"

"Yeah." He stood there looking at me like hey, you know I am playing a video game, right?

"I was thinking of trying to finish it to give it to him. What do you think?"

He shrugged and said, "I think that would be nice." Sam has always had a very kind heart. So, as he went back to his video game, I went to the closet and pulled the train out of my craft tin.

When I took it out of the package and saw its state, I couldn't believe it. With sober eyes, I could see all the mistakes I had made. It was so bad I thought about putting it away but felt the Lord prompting me to finish it.

The process of finishing was quite the journey. Before I could move forward on the project, I needed to go back to correct the mistakes, one piece at a time. Some pieces needed the yarn redone because I had used the wrong color. Some needed to be recut because, you guessed it, I cut it wrong. God was doing work in me while I was working on the train. Every stitch, every mistake, every time I had to undo something and start over, God was teaching me to see the resolution by looking at the problem.

When I finally finished, it wasn't perfect. There were still visible mistakes and imperfections, but with one stitch at a time and one piece at a time, I completed it. It was perfectly imperfect. I put it on the table, admiring it, not knowing if I wanted to part with it, when the Lord broke into my thoughts and said to me, "Jennifer, that train is like your life. You have made some mistakes in your life, but with my help, you can fix them. One at a time, if you keep your hand in mine and walk with me."

I wrote this modern-day parable many years ago, and since then, there have been many ups and downs in my life. Times when life has been so utterly exhilarating, I couldn't imagine living any other life. There have also been other times when I thought I wouldn't make it and felt like giving up because I was so discouraged.

God has shown me that living with discouragement is one of Satan's greatest tools. But what is discouragement? We see the effects of it, but what is it? Quite literally, it is the lack of courage. When I have been discouraged in my life, it has been because I have felt little to no hope in a situation, and when I lack hope, I don't have the courage to get through something, so I become discouraged and stuck.

However, God is faithful, and whenever I feel like that, as I keep seeking him, he does something to uplift me and encourage me. He reminds me that he is still in control, that I can trust him, and as long as my hand is securely in his, I can and will get through anything.

As the Lord and I rebuild my life, the most significant truth I have learned is every life is a miracle that needs to be treasured.

Behold, all things are made new in Christ! Amen.

Did you see yourself in the above parable? Did you catch mistakes that you have made in your life and areas that God wants to fix and make better? It is okay to admit our areas of weakness; that is when God is strongest. When we allow him into our pain and suffering, into the areas that we have kept hidden from him for fear that he will reject us, this is when he turns our valleys of trouble into a gateway of hope.

Isn't it wonderful that we serve a God who is in the habit of rebuilding and restoring lives? He does want to make all things new. In him, we can find comfort and rest for our souls. Our burdens become light, and there is unexplainable joy. The secret, my friend, is staying the course and running the race that the apostle Paul speaks of, with perseverance. When trials and tribulations come, and they will come, know that God goes with us; he walked before us to prepare the way for us.

Gentle Challenge

Today, dear friends, I pose this challenge for you: Find the unfinished train in your life. That project or dream you've shelved away, riddled with mistakes and imperfections. Take it out, dust it off, and finish it one stitch at a time. Who knows what God will reveal to you in the process? Trust him, keep your hand in his, and see what beautiful masterpiece he can create through you. Don't let discouragement hold you back; find courage in Christ and watch as he transforms you.

Reflection Questions

1. In what areas of your life do you recognize the "unfinished train"—a task or dream you started with enthusiasm but left incomplete due to discouragement or fear?

2. How can you apply the metaphor of the "one stitch at a time" process to these unfinished parts of your life, and what steps can you take to start this process?

3. How has your understanding of discouragement and courage changed after reading this piece, and how can you draw strength from Christ in times of discouragement?

Journal Your Thoughts Here

Pray with Me:

Dear heavenly Father,

We come before you today with hearts yearning for guidance and peace. We acknowledge our unfinished trains, those dreams and aspirations that we've shelved due to fear or discouragement. We ask for your wisdom and strength as we endeavor to complete them, one stitch at a time. Please guide us as we seek to correct our mistakes and make amends, just as the train was completed with patience and perseverance. In times of discouragement, remind us that courage comes from relying on you, our Rock and Redeemer. Inspire in us a deeper understanding of your love and faithfulness, turning our discouragement into determination. As we entrust to you these unfinished parts of our lives, may we experience your transformative power, making us more like Christ each day.

In Jesus's name, we pray.

Amen.

Scripture Memory Verse

This means that anyone who belongs to Christ has become a new person. The old life is gone; a new life has begun!

2 Corinthians 5:17 NLT

Endnotes:

1. The author took creative liberties with the gospel message to tell the story in a straight narrative.

2. There is no recorded conversation of the disciples entering the house before Passover.

3. There is no recorded conversation between Caiaphas and Delilah. Delilah is a fictional character made for the retelling of this story.

4. Author added creative conversation talked about in the gospel.

5. Watson, John B., and Rosalie Rayner. "Conditioned Emotional Reactions." Journal of Experimental Psychology, vol. 3, no. 1, 1920, pp. 1–14. doi:10.1037/h0069608

6. Not her real name.

About the Author

Jenn Dafoe-Turner is an author, pastor, speaker, and spiritual midwife who helps others discover freedom and birth their God-given purpose. Her personal story of overcoming addiction and walking in God's grace gives her a unique voice of authenticity and hope. Through her writing and speaking, Jenn comes alongside others with compassion, encouragement, and biblical wisdom, showing that no story is too messy for God to redeem. As a partner at Abundance Books, she equips and empowers authors, speakers, and leaders to share their stories and ministries with confidence and clarity. A graduate of SpeakUp Certification and Christian Speakers Bootcamp, Jenn is also a StrengthsFinder coach and ministry coach who delights in helping people uncover their "why." She lives in Ontario with her husband, Ken, and finds joy in her growing family, especially in being "Memaw" to her grandchildren.

www.ingramcontent.com/pod-product-compliance
Lightning Source LLC
Chambersburg PA
CBHW061758120626
46550CB00005B/2044